Topics on Art and Money

Edited by

Adrià Harillo Pla
Shanghai Jiao Tong University, China

Series in Art

VERNON PRESS

www.vernonpress.com

In the Americas:
Vernon Press
1000 N West Street, Suite 1200
Wilmington, Delaware, 19801
United States

In the rest of the world:
Vernon Press
C/Sancti Espiritu 17,
Malaga, 29006
Spain

Series in Art

Library of Congress Control Number: 2020947808

ISBN: 978-1-64889-048-2

Cover design by Vernon Press using images by Nathan Dumlao and Thomas Dumortie on Unsplash.

Table of Contents

List of Figures

List of Tables

Acknowledgments

Cervantes wrote in his Don Quixote that the worst sin is that of being ungrateful. And I agree with him.

In consequence, I must begin by thanking Vernon Press for publishing this book, contributing to freedom of expression and the divulgation of academic knowledge and research.

I must also thank each of the contributors who have decided to put their trust in the publisher and me to publish their work. I hope this is only the beginning of future academic and personal relationships that will be beneficial to all of us. Therefore, I hope that this book will serve as a beginning for the future.

I also want to thank three university professors who have had an enormous influence on my way of seeing and my academic interests: Gerard Vilar, Adriana Kemp and Titus Levi.

It would not be fair to forget non-university professors who influenced me a lot as a person in my early development, such as Montserrat Pujals or Montserrat Toscano.

People who also deserve a few lines of dedication are all the people I have had the good fortune to meet at congresses, conferences, seminars and other academic events, and who in one way or another have helped me with their constructive criticism and suggestions. One of them, although not the only one, is Francesco Angelini.

I would especially like to thank those people who have no academic but personal relationship with me. This includes my friends: both Marcs, Aida, and Joan. It also includes Ioana, for her love and patience with me. And last but most important: my family, and especially my mother Sara, father Ernesto and sister Címtia.

It is very difficult to name all the people I thank, appreciate, and admire. But I know that they know who they are, beyond what can be written on paper.

Introduction

I have training in the Art Market and also in Philosophy. When you study Philosophy and you have worked in the press, you know that being "neutral" is impossible. Being "neutral" implies getting rid of who you are, your context, your thoughts, your ideology and even your language. However, despite the impossibility of being "neutral," there is something that distinguishes a good philosopher, a good journalist, or a good academic: honesty.

Consequently, I would like to start this book by being honest with both the readers and the contributors who have decided to publish their texts in this book.

When I originally thought about this book, I had a different conception in my head. My initial idea was to prepare a volume based on a libertarian analysis of the current context of the art market. This ideological approach, centered on that specific focus, should have been done from the perspective of Economics, Philosophy, Sociology and any other discipline of interest.

Logically, I presented my idea to a couple of people within the academy for whom I have not only great professional respect, but also personal admiration. One of them said to me: "Okay, go for it, but be careful, sometimes coordinating academics can be like herding cats." Far from it, the initial idea was very well accepted but above all, I discovered the high level of proposals from people who had common interests with mine: the relationship between art and money. The mutual recognition of these common interests greatly facilitated the entire process.

It is completely true that, in some cases, the contributors of this book may not share my ideology, perspective or opinions, but the scientific rigor and the solidity of their work made me remember two things. Firstly, that coordinating a book like this is a great honor and, above all, a great responsibility. Secondly, that nothing is more libertarian than allowing people to express themselves without limiting their ideas to a specific line of thought. Through their diverse work with a common background idea—that of art and money—the contributors of this book have reminded me what libertarianism is and, at the same time, taught me a lot from that relation, each of them from their line of specialization. I have already learned many things while preparing this book, and I hope that its readers will also do so through reading it.

Thus, this book consists of 7 chapters that, from an economic, historical, cultural or political perspective, for example, somehow reflect that relationship between art and money.

In fact, the title of this book is also intended to be an honest title far from bombastic phrases and empty meanings. And from honesty, the chosen one is made up of three words, a preposition and a coordinating conjunction: Topics on Art and Money.

A coordinating conjunction, not a subordinating one, since this book does not intend to express a hierarchical order. As all words are united by a coordinating conjunction, this book intends to connect them. "And" connects; "or" divides. In turn, this book does not pretend to present only some ways in which art and money are linked, but between academics from different fields and geographical areas as well.

It is completely true that even nowadays some people still deny the existence of that relationship. It is not that they consider it appropriate or not, fair or not, desirable or not; it is simply that they deny such a connection. This position seems unrealistic. Since ancient times, thinkers such as Aristotle defended that money was a conventional common measure that refers to everything and with which everything is measured. Art is a part of the whole that we are, as humans and society. This money is what allows for the allocation of resources within human communities, and therefore, in every human community with something named art, art and money connect in one way or another.

In fact—and if I may use a literary reference—there is a beautiful text written by Leonard E. Read called "I, pencil." In that short text, a simple pencil explains the complexity of its creation and how no one in the whole world knows completely how to make him; how human interconnections are key, from the beginning to the end, to its creation, sale, and use. Money would be the fundamental element in the coordination of all the people who, without knowing each other, are involved in the creation of this pencil. Something as basic as a pencil needs an element as human as money is. The artist needs a pencil to draw, to create or to sketch. The curator needs to write his explanation for an exhibition and, the critic, for his assessment. How could we reject the relationship between art and money? We simply cannot, even in the most basic level of ideas. We can differ, however, in how we see it, we value it, or we apply it, and this book is an honest way to present some of them.

Chapter 1

From Nodes to Nudes

Kevin Xiong

Independent Scholar

Abstract

This three-part study establishes a significant and positive relationship between an artist's affiliation with galleries holding diverse and influential portfolios and her subsequent success at auction. The paper finds that an artist's financial success in the secondary market, measured by annual auction sales and maximum auction prices, can be predicted by looking at the network importance of that artist's galleries—via a multiple regression model incorporating network statistics like weighted degree centrality, eigenvector centrality, and clustering coefficients. It also tests an instrument, sudden shifts in network location due to exogenous gallery closings (e.g., Knoedler Gallery's sudden closure over fraud allegations). The instrument yields positive and significant results in 18 out of 32 instrumental variable regressions, a promising step toward establishing causality. This paper brings insights from the world's largest artwork dataset to an emerging body of literature leveraging network tools in art market analyses. Additionally, the background section offers a structural overview of the art market based on expert interviews and a literature review. I conclude the paper with a dive into the study's limitations and a concrete list of potential extensions and considerations for future research.

Keywords: Centrality; instrument; networks; regression; valuation.

* * *

1. Introduction

"Who pays $12 million for a decaying shark?" asks economist Donald Thompson in "The $12 Million Stuffed Shark" (Thompson 2012, 4). The title of Thompson's bestseller references none other than Damien Hirst's 1991 installation, "The Physical Impossibility of Death in the Mind of Someone Living," a tiger shark soaked in formaldehyde that in January 2005 set the record for the second greatest sum of money ever paid for a work by a living artist (Thompson 2012, 1-2). Why all the commotion over a second-place sale?[1]

Something about a fish without chips left the public as sour as lemons: Hirst's "Impossibility" drew an unprecedented level of public criticism. Art critic Robert Hughes labeled it a "cultural obscenity" (Kennedy 2004). "The string of brush marks in a lace collar in a Velázquez painting could be more radical," he quipped, "[than a shark] murkily disintegrating in its tank on the other side of the Thames" (Kennedy 2004). The Stuckists, an art activist group whose primary goal is to protest the legitimacy of conceptual art, simultaneously held a counter-exhibition at their gallery entitled "A Dead Shark Isn't Art" when Hirst's work went on display (Stuckism International Gallery 2020). Hirst often gets the ubiquitous contemporary art reaction—"I could do that"—to which he retorts: "But you didn't, did you?" (Barber 2003).

Don Thompson, the author whose question opens this paper, raises an age-old question: what determines the price of an artwork, if not the intrinsic qualities of the artwork? It is likely that many factors—institutional affiliations, collector history, auction environments, clever marketing, size, medium—play a part in the process. How do we test their importance? How do we quantify their contribution to an artwork's price at auction?

This paper focuses on one particular factor, an artist's gallery affiliations, and finds they have a significant and positive relationship with her performance at auction. Specifically, I examine the "network importance" of an artist's galleries by constructing a weighted, monopartite network of art galleries connected by shared artists—network statistics like degree centrality, betweenness, and closeness serve as proxies for diverse and influential gallery portfolios. I then test the relationship between "network importance" and auction performance using three tools: hypothesis testing, log-level regression, and an instrumental variable—sudden and exogenous gallery closings leading to shifts in network location. All three methods point to the same conclusion: the way in which an artist's gallery is connected to other galleries has significant implications for her financial success.

This study is among the first to bring network tools to the art valuation analyses and involves the most comprehensive dataset on the global art network to date from Artsy. This research contributes to academic discussions on artwork valuation and provenance through a network-based approach that quantifies many of the sociological variables discussed in existing literature,

---

[1] Jasper Johns' 1954 *Flag* held first place at the time.

like whether an artist's gallery is reputable or whether an artist's galleries are likely to collaborate with each other.

2. Background & Literature Review

A primer on artists, galleries, and other art world constituents

Artists form relationships with galleries for numerous reasons, but the foundational reason is commercial: to sell their work. Three kinds of artist-gallery relationships emerge: formal representation, collection, and consignment.

The majority of established artists will seek formal representation—though the term "formal" is used loosely here—through contracts, handshake deals, and gentlemen's agreements with galleries who will help them sell their work in exchange for a cut of their sales.[2] The arrangements vary significantly, with typical galleries keeping anywhere from 33% to 44% of the revenues from a sale and top commercial galleries commanding even more, up to 60% (Zorloni 2005, 62). Galleries justify these impressive margins with the notion that they contribute the capital needed to store and display their work and cultivate the success of their artists. Galleries will frequently promote their artists, bring works to art fairs, print catalogs, and tap into their network of art collectors and dealers. Galleries may even provide artists with studio space and living stipends.

Outside of formal representation, there is the second type of artist-gallery affiliation: collection. This refers to galleries taking stock in other artists' work, often by acquiring them in the secondary market, at auction, or from art dealers, in hopes that the work's value will appreciate over time for resale.[3] Many established artists are formally represented by galleries and simultaneously see their work owned and sold by other galleries. For example, a number of galleries sell the work of Felix Gonzalez-Torres, but Andrea Rosen Gallery in New York has formally represented him since 1990 (Andrea Rosen Gallery 2020).

The third type of artist-gallery affiliation is inter-gallery collaboration via consignment, in which one gallery may represent an artist on behalf of another gallery, both taking a cut of the sales.[4] A gallery in London may think that one

[2] Jessica Backus (Artsy, Senior Director of Marketplace Strategy and Operations), interview with author, February 9, 2017.

[3] Shalimar Fojas White (Herman and Joan Suit Librarian, Harvard FAS Fine Arts Library), interview with author, October 18, 2016.

[4] White, interview with author.

of its artists would sell better in the Los Angeles regional art market and work with a gallery there to curate an exhibit. Critical acclaim and better branding may also motivate collaboration via consignment: a blue-chip gallery with more resources and loyal collectors may see many benefits to partnering with a younger gallery with more street credibility or critical acclaim.[5]

Note that in all three types of artist-gallery affiliation, gallery and artist financial incentives appear directionally aligned—both parties aim to increase their profits, and their collaboration presumably benefits everyone. Between galleries, on the other hand, the incentives are slightly foggier. In the first category of formal representation, a gallery likely does not want its artists to simultaneously seek representation elsewhere, as that divides the amount of work each gallery is able to sell. However, if the other representing gallery is highly reputable and boosts the provenance of all the artist's work, perhaps collaboration is beneficial. With a collection, a gallery's incentives to take stock in an artist's work similarly may vary, depending on which other galleries also own work by the artist. Only in consignment do the incentives to collaborate between galleries seem aligned. While this paper supports the idea that, all else held equal, galleries who share artists with other galleries see stronger auction sales for their artists, it does not endorse an oversimplification of the incentives that shape connectivity among galleries.

On the demand side, the buyers that make up the largely unregulated art market are diverse in age, nationality, industry, taste, and intention. Together, these buyers generate over $60 billion in global sales per year, with the United States, United Kingdom, and China forming 43%, 21%, and 19% of the market, respectively (Kinsella 2016). Trends in this population will often dictate the direction of the art market. For example, Chinese works have risen in popularity in the past decade. This trend has led to the breakout of Chinese artists, new gallery openings in Beijing, Shanghai, Hong Kong, and stronger Chinese artist representation in galleries with a good pulse on market trends.[6] There are also those who buy art as an alternative asset. Disapproving art world citizens have coined the term "flippers" to describe buyers who resell works quickly after their purchase to turn a quick profit (Kazakina 2014). Many large financial institutions run art investment funds for sophisticated clients. Auction houses like Sotheby's and Christie's act as a secondary market and help art buyers acquire works from those looking to sell.

An artist's financial success is often measured by their performance at auction, rather than through gallery sales. Data on the latter is opaque and

---

[5] Backus, interview with author.

[6] White, interview with author.

difficult to access, even though such data may be more representative of demand for the artist's most current work in the primary market. Secondary sales at auction create 53% of the art market's value, relative to 47% created by other sales (Kinsella 2016).

Other constituents in the art market complicate this picture of artist, gallery, and auction house. Art dealers, critics, curators, advisors, and art fairs play an important role in facilitating transactions, shaping consumer tastes, and supplementing (or circumnavigating) the artist-gallery-auction house triangle—though they are beyond the scope of this paper. Additional edge cases and exceptions abound: sometimes an artist (usually a very famous one, like Damien Hirst) will bypass galleries and sell their works directly at auction. Auction houses have also begun to open their own commercial galleries (Wang 2013).

This paper focuses on the more traditional and ubiquitous relationships between artist, gallery, and auction house. It considers how a "well-connected" gallery portfolio might predict how its artists subsequently perform at an auction. A great deal of literature has attempted to explain the significant variables that lead to a stronger performance at auction for artists. These variables range from artist-related qualities like age, nationality, medium, and movement to external qualities like provenance and gallery reputation.

What goes into artwork pricing?

Art world scholars like Rengers, Velthuis, Schonfeld, and Reinstaller have begun a conversation on the different factors that contribute to artwork pricing. Rengers and Velthuis, in "Determinants of Prices for Contemporary Art in Dutch Galleries, 1992-1998," find that, in addition to other determinants like size and material of work, the artist's age is a key factor in pricing in the Dutch art market (Rengers and Velthuis 2002). The study notes that the prices a gallery can command from its works depend more on characteristics of the gallery's represented artists, like their ages, than on characteristics of the gallery itself (Rengers and Velthuis 2002, 24). Schönfeld and Reinstaller run a similar model on the primary art market and also find that artist career length, comparable to artist age, has a positive correlation with sale price, but that other coefficients like artist professorship and gallery reputation are not statistically significant (Schönfeld and Reinstaller 2007, 152). These two studies attribute successful commercial performance to artist, rather than gallery, characteristics.

In contrast, popular accounts of exorbitantly priced artworks like Don Thompson's "The $12 Million Stuffed Shark" point to a work's institutional affiliations and provenance, among other factors like intelligent branding and irrational bidding behavior at auctions, as key factors in artwork pricing (Thompson 2012). Thompson asserts that Damien Hirst's formaldehyde-soaked shark broke records at auction largely thanks to the prestige and coordination of its previous homes: Gagosian Gallery, Saatchi Gallery, and the Royal Academy of Arts in London. Collaboration and branding between these institutions and the artist, Thompson argues, was what created value for the work (Thompson 2012).

Campos and Barbosa's "Paintings and numbers: an econometric investigation of sales rates, prices, and returns in Latin American art auctions" also pushes back on Schönfeld and Reinstaller. Campos and Barbosa discuss omitted variables in Rengers and Velthuis's study and offer a strong argument in favor of provenance's role in predicting artwork pricing. The duo examines a hand-coded dataset of 1640 paintings in Sotheby's Latin American Art Auctions from 1995 to 2002 (Campos and Barbosa 2009, 29). In their methodology, they create three dummy variables to account for provenance: "catalogue raisonné" (if the work appears in the scholarly listing of an artist's work), "artbook" (whether Sotheby's reports the work's reproduction in a reputable book), and "exhibited" (whether the work was selected as part of a prominent museum or gallery exhibition). The authors find that these three provenance-related indicators are "crucially important" predictors of pricing—more important than medium, size, and expert opinion—with each variable significant at the 1% level (Campos and Barbosa 2009, 45-49). Qualitative discussion of art markets like the work of Alessia Zorloni validates these findings, describing museums and cultural institutions as important "validators" of good art "in the absence of objective standards of certification" (Zorloni 2005, 67).

My study picks up where Campos, Barbosa, and Zorloni's work left off. While they make robust claims about the importance of provenance in forecasting Sotheby's auction prices, further investigation into the institutions that endow an artwork with provenance is needed. Who are these institutions? From what do they derive their prestige and influence? This paper uses network importance as one potential proxy for provenance, asserting that galleries derive their influence from their network location, which then has implications for their artists' valuations at auction.

Applying network analysis to art pricing

Obtaining art world data for network analysis is an optimal approach to answering these questions—though a somewhat nascent one. In this section, I provide an overview of how network tools have been applied to discourses outside and inside the art world to demonstrate that this paper is novel in both its methodology (correlating network statistics with commercial outcomes) and the scale of artwork data it employs.

Outside the art world, network analysis as a means of understanding phenomena abounds. Amaral, Scala, Barthelemy, and Stanley detect small-world networks in movie-actor collaborations, neurons of worms, and Gcitations of scientific papers (Amaral 2000). Kogut and Walker, in "The Small World of Germany and the Durability of National Networks," similarly find that levels of clustering among a diverse network of 550 German firms connected by common owners can predict acquisition decisions (Kogut and Walker 2001, 332).

In the art world, network analyses are rarer, but three sets of scholars have begun to bring network tools to valuation-adjacent discussions at a local scale. Braden uses centrality measures to assess the "cultural consecration" of 125 Armory and MoMA-exhibited artists through the number of pages they occupy across three 21st-century art history textbooks (Braden 2018). He finds that "exhibition-created networks are important to an artist's subsequent attention in art history" and that "those not only well-connected, but also strongly connected, are likely to attract long-term recognition" (Braden 2018, 16). Etro and Stepanova use network analysis and distribution of master-student degree centralities to find that, among 1,906 Dutch and Flemish painters, the probability of any given master having k students can be modeled with a scale-free network (Etro and Stepanova 2018, 217-222). In other words, talented painters like Rembrandt and Rubens were able to attract and train many more followers than ordinary painters. A third scholar is Giuffre, who compiles a dataset of 159 contemporary photographers with gallery affiliations between 1981 and 1992 and correlates affiliation with one of three clusters emerging from the network (the independent variables) with the number of reviews a given photographer receives in "ArtNews" and "Art in America" over the same time period, a proxy for critical success (the dependent variable) (Giuffre 1999). Giuffre finds that "those who have had a long history of membership in loosely knit networks" receive more critical consideration than artists in "tightly knit cliques" and those with "sporadic connections to the art world" (Giuffre 1999, 815). These three sets of scholars provide the foundation for this paper in how they apply network tools to art world datasets. However, this work furthers their research by expanding the N to over 50,000 artists; controlling for numerous other indicators, including nationality, age, and medium; and merging network data with auction data as a measure of commercial success. As Giuffre notes, "measuring artists' success in monetary terms is difficult owing to a lack of information" (Giuffre 1999, 826); this paper meaningfully overcomes this challenge.

The paper that perhaps has come closest to measuring how networks affect commercial success in the art world is Brian Uzzi and Jarret Spiro's "Collaboration and Creativity: The Small World Problem." They take a network approach to analyzing a dataset of 2,092 composers, lyricists, directors, choreographers, and other creative individuals who worked on musicals together between 1945 and 1989. The authors find that, up to a certain "bliss point" Q, the presence of clusters in the network can predict a Broadway production's financial and critical success (Uzzi and Spiro 2005, 447). In their study, Q represents a "small world quotient," which is a ratio of two ratios: a network's clustering coefficient over that of a random graph to a network's average path length over that of a random graph (Uzzi and Spiro 2005, 453). A higher Q means the clusters within a network are more connected (i.e., there are many edges connecting cluster to cluster). If Q is too high, a network may become too connected and cohesive for innovation; if Q is too low, then creative ideas may not spread at all (Uzzi and Spiro 2005, 464). "Clusters of interacting artists help incubate conventions. At the same time, between-cluster connections increase the likelihood that different conventions will come into contact" (Uzzi and Spiro 2005, 462). Using box office and critic reviews data on the 442 musicals these artists were involved in, they find that a medium Q score is what leads to box office success and high reviews (Uzzi and Spiro 2005, 467). The authors' use of bipartite affiliation networks—creative individuals and the shows on which they collaborate—is comparable to the bipartite nature of this study's art institution network of art institutions and all the artists they represent. Additionally, while this paper does not construct Q scores for the art world, I do seek to connect network statistics to the commercial success of creative works.

3. Data

Part I: Network Data

The network data in this study comes from Artsy, the world's largest online art database. With over 50,000 artists and 500,000 artworks, it is the leading resource for art collecting and education, working to bring all the world's art online (Artsy 2017). The obtained dataset is a two-column array of artist-gallery pairs, spanning 88,119 rows. The data form a bipartite network consisting of artists and galleries and the directed edges that connect them, indicating representation. I conduct a significant clean-up operation to remove anonymous private collections and to correct typos in artist and gallery names. Ultimately, I transform the directed bipartite network into an undirected monopartite network of galleries as nodes, connected by weighted edges equal to the count of shared artists between each pair of galleries (See Appendix A). To do this, I use Gephi, a network analysis and visualization tool.

After constructing an undirected monopartite network, I use Gephi functions to calculate the following network statistics: degree centrality, weighted degree centrality, closeness centrality, betweenness centrality, eigenvector centrality,

PageRank centrality, clustering coefficient, and weighted clustering coefficient. These statistics are briefly described below:

- **Degree and weighted degree centralities**: Degree centrality is a count of the number of edges stemming from a node, and a weighted degree is simply the sum of the weights of each of those edges. These two measures of centrality assign importance to nodes which have many neighbors and strong connections to them. In the context of this paper, degree centrality lends importance to institutions who share artists with many other institutions.

- **Closeness centrality:** Instead of counting edges like degree centrality, closeness centrality looks at geography. "Closeness," in this case, is the reciprocal of the average distance, or "farness," between a given node and every other node in the network. Institutions that are well-connected to other institutions through a small number of degrees of separation are considered important in this centrality calculation.

- **Betweenness centrality**: Betweenness centrality calculates the fraction of times a node lies on the shortest path between two other nodes in the network. For example, a betweenness centrality of 0 means that the node lies on none of the shortest paths in the network, and a betweenness centrality of 1 means the node lies on all of them. In the context of the art world, a node with high betweenness might be an important mecca through which important art market insights pass.

- **Eigenvector and PageRank centralities:** These centrality measures assign scores iteratively to each node in the network based on the importance of the other nodes to which it is connected.

- **Clustering coefficient and weighted clustering coefficient:** The local clustering coefficient represents the proportion of all possible connections among nodes in a node's neighborhood that are realized in the form of closed triplets (or triangles). In other words, if a node is connected to three other nodes, and all of those nodes are also connected to each other, then three out of three possible triplets are closed, and the clustering coefficient is 1. An extension to the local clustering coefficient, the local weighted clustering coefficient Gephi computes is based on the calculation proposed in Barrat et al.'s 2004 paper, which incorporates the weights of the edges between a given node and its neighbors (Barrat et al. 2004, 3750).

Part II: Auction Data

As this study draws connections between network properties and artist performance at auction, I also require artist-level auction data. I use Artnet's expansive auction results database, obtained via an Artnet analytics report. The dataset contains total sales and maximum auction prices across three years (2013 through 2015) for each artist, in addition to descriptive information like year of birth, nationality, primary medium, and whether the artist is deceased.

Indicator variables: I generate indicator variables for year of sales (2014 and 2015), each medium (acrylic, oil, tempera, ink, watercolor, print, sculpture, mixed media, drawing, and photograph), and nationality (American, Chinese, Japanese, Italian, Indian, French, Russian, German, Spanish, British, Mexican, Brazilian, Turkish, Swiss, and Swedish). For the year of sales, 2013 becomes the base category of the indicator variable. Media and nationalities not mentioned are the base categories for their respective groups. For ease of interpretation, I generate a variable for each artist's age at the time of observation by subtracting her year of birth from the year of sale.

Part III: Combining Network Statistics, Auction Data, and Artist Characteristics

I join the Artnet data to the Artsy data on a column of artist names, bringing my combined dataset to 14,135 observations. To ensure a comprehensive join, I manually standardize spelling, accents, and capitalization of artist names between the two datasets, though this introduces some room for human error, discussed further in "Limitations."

By taking the median or maximum of each artist's affiliated institutions' network statistics, I calculate the following 18 artist-level statistics: median degree centrality, maximum degree centrality, median weighted degree centrality, maximum weighted degree, median closeness centrality, maximum closeness centrality, median betweenness centrality, maximum betweenness centrality, median eigenvector centrality, maximum eigenvector centrality, median PageRank centrality, maximum PageRank centrality, median clustering coefficient, maximum clustering coefficient, median weighted clustering coefficient, and maximum weighted clustering coefficient. I calculate medians in lieu of means to avoid potential issues with outliers, such as affiliation with an institution that commands a markedly greater number of degrees than all the others. I include maximum statistics to allow for the possibility that an artist's auction performance is better determined by their most important gallery, as opposed to the median level of importance across their galleries.

Summary statistics: The mean and median sum of sales for any given artist in my dataset are $1.5 million and $34,603, respectively, in any given year between 2013 and 2015. The mean maximum auction price is $428,824, compared to a median of $16,250. The gaps between means and medians point to a strongly positively skewed set of outcome variables, further corroborated by the distribution plots in Figures 1.1a-b. As a result, I log transform the sum of sales and maximum auction price in the "Methods" section. The other summary statistics paint a fuller picture of the data. The median artist is 74 years old. The median gallery representing, consigning, or taking stock in an artist is connected to 244 (using the arithmetic mean) or 161 (using the median) other galleries through shared artists. Overall, this final sample of 14,135 represents a high achieving group of artists who are associated with well-connected galleries.

Survival bias is worth noting in this sample. Only the artists who are prominent enough to have their work uploaded to Artsy or auction results recorded by Artnet survive the journey to this joined dataset.

Figure 1.1a | Distributions of Auction Performance Variables

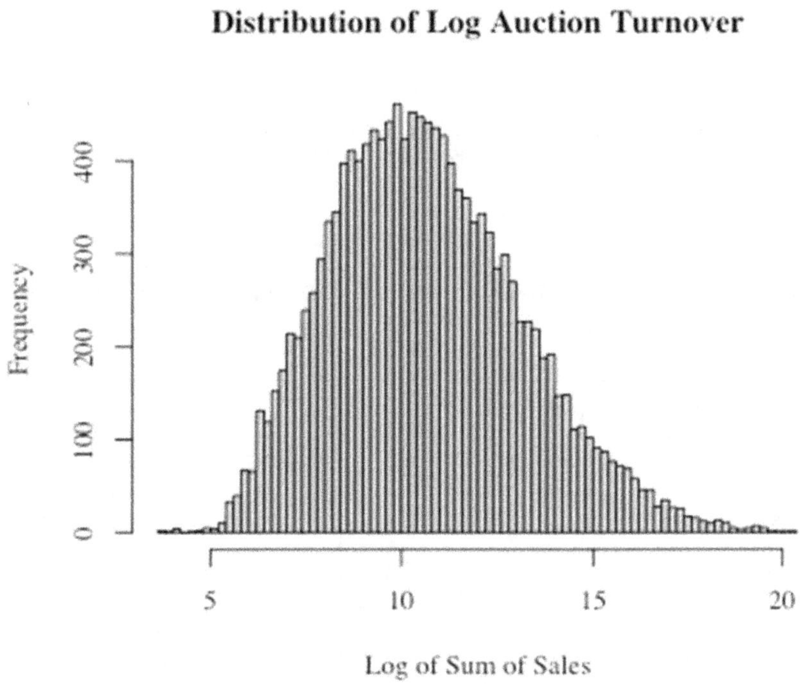

Figure 1.1b | Distributions of Auction Performance Variables

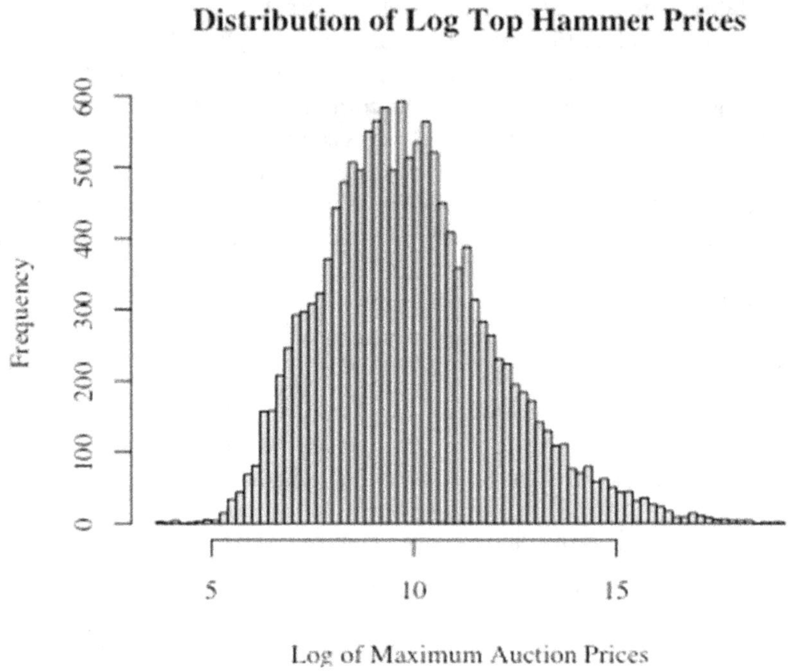

The paper's two outcome variables, auction turnover (the sum of an artist's sales) and top hammer prices (the maximum price an artist achieved at auction), are both strongly and positively skewed. Consequently, they are log-transformed.

Table 1.1 | Summary Statistics

Statistic	*Mean*	*Median*	*St. Dev.*	*Min*	*Max*
Sum of Sales	1,543,730	34,603	13,659,703	38	651,393,080
Maximum Auction Price	428,824	16,250	3,787,968	38	179,365,000
Age	99.276	74	94.525	4	1,693
Median Degree	243.726	161	272.807	0	1,158.00
Max Degree	447.271	318	407.786	0	1,163
Median Weighted Degree	638.659	219.5	1,172.32	0	5,282.00
Max Weighted Degree	1,471.03	481	1,848.55	0	5,488
Median Closeness	0.426	0.437	0.075	0	0.556

Max Closeness	0.457	0.463	0.086	0	0.558
Median Betweenness	0.003	0.001	0.007	0	0.033
Max Betweenness	0.007	0.002	0.01	0	0.033
Median Clustering Coefficient	0.363	0.351	0.156	0	1
Max Clustering Coefficient	0.479	0.467	0.222	0	1
Median Weighted CC	0.422	0.421	0.156	0	1
Max Weighted CC	0.525	0.515	0.211	0	1
Median PageRank	0.001	0.0004	0.002	0.00004	0.008
Max PageRank	0.002	0.001	0.003	0.00004	0.008
Median Eigenvector	0.257	0.176	0.257	0	0.981
Max Eigenvector	0.438	0.383	0.358	0	1

Summary statistics reveal a sample of high-achieving artists, whose mean sales exceed $1.5 million (USD). Survival bias may explain this.

4. Methods

After a significant data clean-up effort and analysis of summary statistics, I employ a set of statistical and econometric tools to support my hypothesis testing, multiple regression, and IV regressions. I outline my methodology in eight steps below.

1. **Log transformation of outcome variables:** Both of the outcome variables, sum of sales and maximum auction price, are strongly right-skewed, so I take a natural log of each to help normalize their distributions.

2. **Hypothesis testing**: I conduct hypothesis testing on each network-related explanatory variable to test whether network statistics demonstrate promise in predicting auction performance. Some explanatory variables behave differently when included in a multiple linear regression due to multicollinearity. This exploratory step isolates the variables to determine whether they have predictive power on their own.

3. **Initial regression:** I begin constructing models of auction success by regressing each of the two dependent variables (auction turnover and top hammer prices) on all explanatory variables and check that the F-statistics are significant at the 5% level, indicating that at least one of the explanatory variables is needed in each model.

4. **Correlation matrix**: I generate a correlation matrix consisting of all explanatory variables, finding that maximum and median statistics are highly correlated. Consequently, I generate two models, one for maximum statistics and another for median statistics, for each of the dependent variables. I remove additional collinear explanatory variables within each model.

5. **Backward stepwise regression**: I select my final model through backward stepwise regression, using Akaike Information Criterion (AIC), for all four models, ultimately settling on ones that include only variables significant at the 5% level.

6. **Interaction variables**: I explore several interaction variables to test more nuanced relationships, with the goal of generating a better model of auction performance.

7. **Outliers and influential points**: I use a Cook's distance D_i cutoff for each model to identify and remove influential points. I employ the commonly used cutoff of $D_i > 4/(N - k - 1)$, where N is the number of observations and k is the number of explanatory variables. This cutoff represents a more "conservative measure" ideal for large datasets like this one (Pearson Prentice 2020).

8. **IV regression**: While multiple linear regression and hypothesis testing reveal significant and positive correlations between well-connected gallery portfolios and artist auction performance, they do not dictate a causal relationship between the two. In an attempt to test whether my predicted direction of causality holds true, I examine sudden network location changes via exogenous gallery closings through an IV regression to mitigate the presence of reverse causality and omitted variable bias. Using art world news sources like "Artnet," "Artnews," and "ArtForum," I assemble a

sample of recently closed galleries.[7] For each of these gallery artists, I compare the year of auction performance immediately after a gallery closes to the year leading up to the closing. This produced a sample of 29 artists whom these galleries formally represented, collected, or consigned. For each gallery, I re-run network statistics for all the nodes in the network after removing the closed gallery to simulate what the network would look like after the exogenous gallery closing, assuming no other changes in the network. At the artist-level, I calculate medians and maxima across the artist's affiliated galleries to reflect the artist's change in network location in the year after closing. Through an IV regression, I attempt to quantify how sudden changes in network location for an artist influence their subsequent auction performance.

5. Results

Part I: Hypothesis Testing

I begin my exploration of the explanatory power of network statistics through hypothesis testing. In each test, I regress the response variables on the explanatory variable of interest. If the coefficient of the explanatory variable is significant at the 5% level, I find sufficient evidence to reject the null hypothesis that the explanatory variable in question has no significant predictive power in estimating auction performance. In 29 out of 32 hypothesis tests, I find significant evidence to reject the null hypothesis. In other words, all of my network statistics are significantly and positively correlated with increases in auction turnover and top hammer prices, with the exception of three relationships: log of sum of sales and median betweenness, log of sum of sales and median clustering coefficient, and log of maximum auction price and median clustering coefficient. Table 1.2 documents the results of these 32 hypothesis tests. In this initial exploration, I see that network statistics demonstrate great promise as predictors of auction performance.

[7] The galleries in my sample consist of Yvon Lambert (the 68-year-old owner decided to retire and focus on his private collection), Knoedler Gallery (closed suddenly over fraud allegations), Salander O'Reilly (closed suddenly over a theft lawsuit), McKee Gallery (cited disappointment in the "changing art world"), and Mike Weiss Gallery (closed due to injurious construction next door).

Table 1.2 | Hypothesis Testing

	Log of Sum of Sales	*Log of Maximum Auction Price*
Median Degree	0.001*** (0.0001)	0.001*** (0.0001)
Max Degree	0.002*** (0.00005)	0.002*** (0.00004)
Median Weighted Degree	0.0001*** (0.00002)	0.0001*** (0.00002)
Max Weighted Degree	0.001*** (0.00001)	0.0004*** (0.00001)
Median Closeness	5.049*** (0.277)	4.219*** (0.238)
Max Closeness	7.822*** (0.234)	6.526*** (0.202)
Median Betweenness	-1.408 (2.974)	-4.299* (2.553)
Max Betweenness	71.041*** (1.914)	58.372*** (1.65)
Median PageRank	87.755*** (12.696)	63.957*** (10.903)
Max PageRank	356.819*** (7.629)	295.218*** (6.584)
Median Eigenvector	1.953*** (0.08)	1.602*** (0.069)
Max Eigenvector	2.519*** (0.055)	2.080*** (0.047)
Median Clustering Coefficient	0.149 (0.134)	0.114 (0.115)
Max Clustering Coefficient	2.802*** (0.092)	2.305*** (0.079)
Median Weighted CC	1.417*** (0.134)	1.150*** (0.115)
Max Weighted CC	3.197*** (0.096)	2.639*** (0.083)

Note: Standard errors are in parentheses. Each coefficient in this table corresponds to a simple linear regression. "CC" is an abbreviation for clustering coefficient. Note that 29 out of 32 hypothesis tests yield significant and positive results. *$p<0.1$; **$p<0.05$; ***$p<0.01$

Part II: Models for Auction Turnover and Maximum Auction Price

I move from hypothesis testing to more comprehensive artist valuation models by employing multiple regression tools: removing collinear variables, log transforming the outcome variables, dropping outliers, and controlling for qualitative variables like age, medium, and nationality.

Initial regressions of total auction turnover and maximum auction price on all explanatory variables yield F-statistics of 29 and 27, respectively, both significant at the 5% level, indicating that at least one of the explanatory variables is needed. However, many of the network-related variables in these two models are not significant, potentially because the network statistics are highly correlated with each other. Consequently, I generate correlation matrices to refine this model of auction performance.

Indeed, the correlation matrix of all network statistics reveals a great degree of collinearity between medians and maxima of the same type of network statistics, such as median and maximum closeness centrality. The correlation matrix also shows that network statistics are overwhelmingly positively correlated with each other, with the exception of clustering coefficients (abbreviated as "CC" in Figures 1.2a-b), as each is a different type of measurement of network importance.

As a result, I build two models for each of the two outcome variables, one for median statistics and one for maximum statistics, further omitting collinear network variables within each model, using the correlation matrices in Figures 1.3 and 1.4 as references. These four models later become eight as I incorporate interaction variables (see Table 1.3 and Table 1.4). Ultimately, I select only degree centrality and clustering coefficient as my network-related variables in each model to minimize collinearity and ensure consistency across models for ease of comparison. My final models are presented in the following sections, after log transformations of the outcome variables, backward stepwise regression, Cook's distance treatments, and the incorporation of various controls and interaction variables.

Figure 1.2a | Correlation Matrix of All Network Statistics

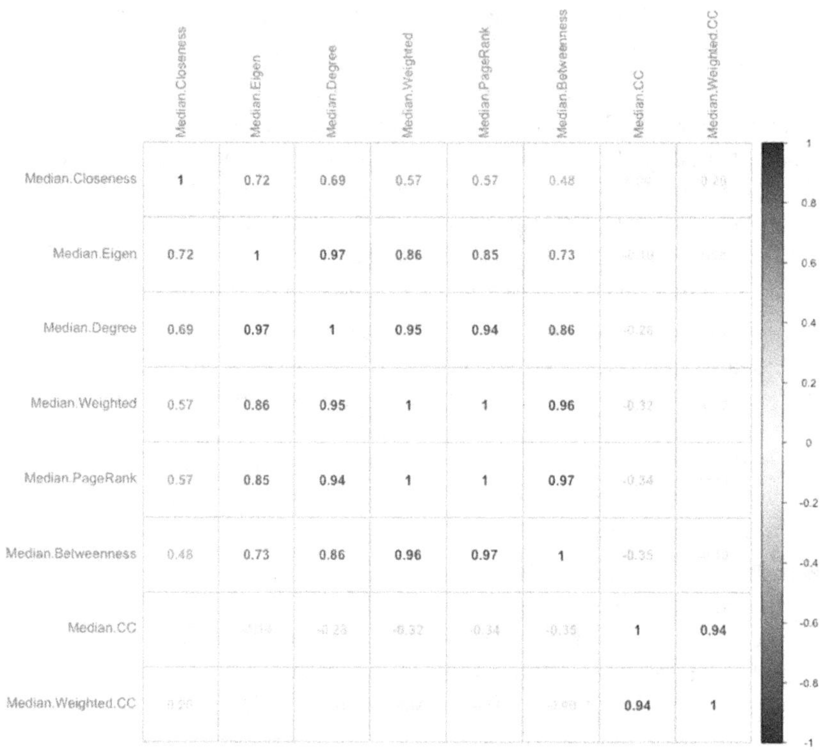

Network statistics are highly correlated with each other, with the exception of clustering coefficients (abbreviated as "CC"), as each is a different type of measurement of network importance.

Figure 1.2b | Correlation Matrix of All Network Statistics

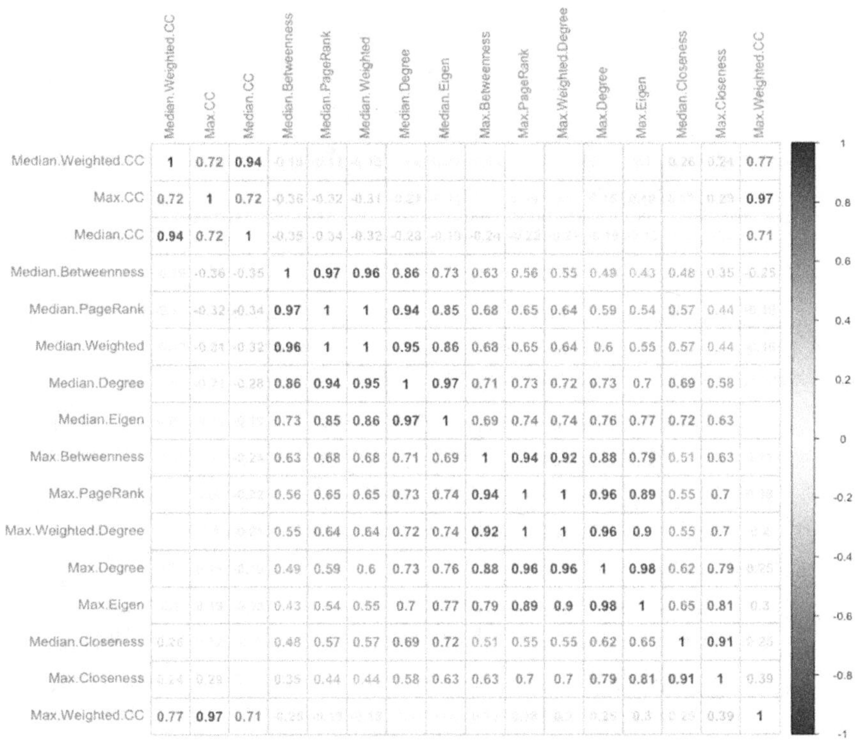

Network statistics are highly correlated with each other, with the exception of clustering coefficients (abbreviated as "CC"), as each is a different type of measurement of network importance.

Figure 1.3 | Correlation Matrix of Median Network Statistics

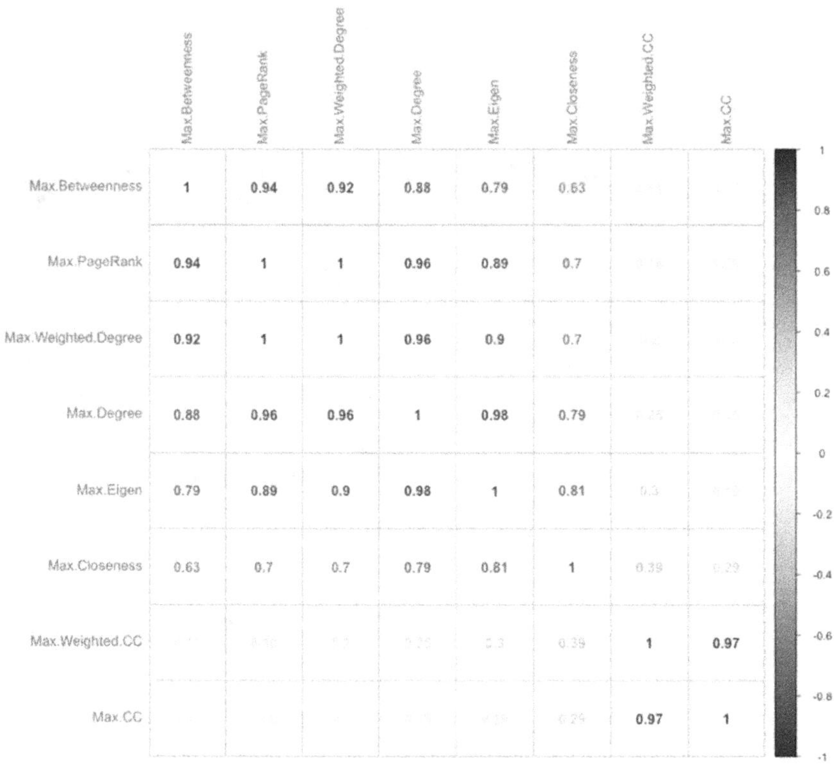

Even after narrowing to only median network statistics, collinearity among the variables persists.

Figure 1.4 | Correlation Matrix of Max Network Statistics

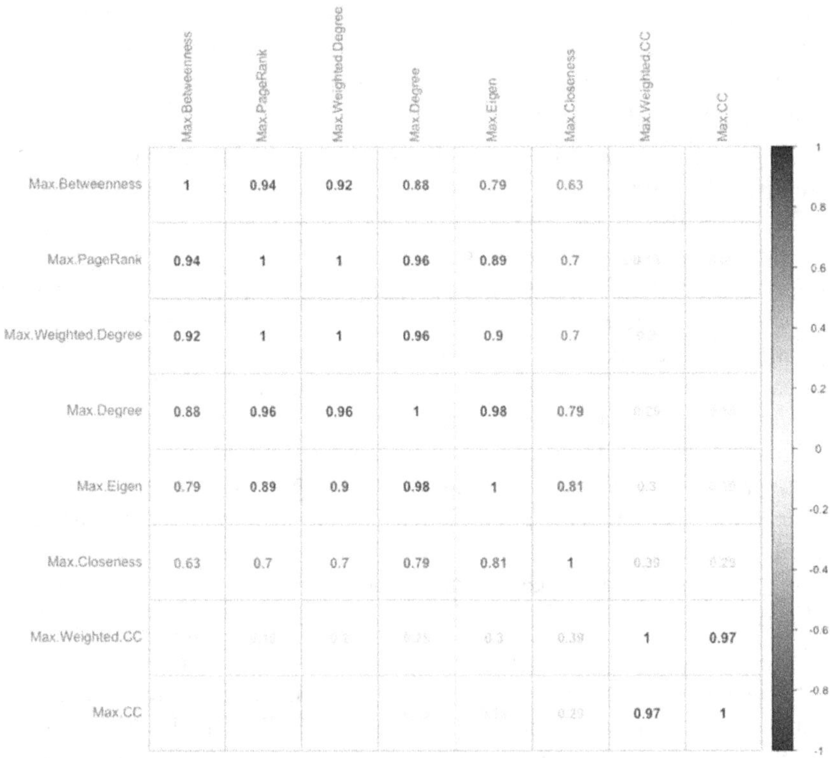

Even after narrowing to only maximum network statistics, collinearity among the variables persists.

Sum of Sales Models

My sum of sales models based on median and maximum network statistics (including interaction variables) account for 15% and 32%, respectively, of the variation in response data: the natural logarithm of total sales in a year at auction for an artist. Both models confirm my hypothesis that network statistics, as proxies for the diversification and connectedness of a gallery's artist portfolio, can provide a powerful basis for understanding artist valuations at auction. The second log-level regression, involving maximum network statistics, appears to be a more robust model of total artist sales given its greater coefficient of determination R^2. Nonetheless, both models contribute valuable insights into gallery networks and artist valuation.

The model incorporating median network statistics sees positive and significant coefficients for median degree centrality and median clustering coefficient. This indicates that artists affiliated with galleries that have, on average, more connections to other galleries in the network via artist representation see a stronger performance at auction. An increase in median degree centrality by one unit, for example, predicts a 0.3% increase in sales at auction in my second model incorporating interactions.

A significant negative coefficient on the interaction between median degree centrality and whether the artist is deceased adds more nuance to the otherwise positive relationship between degree centrality and stronger sales. Deceased artists affiliated with galleries that represent many other well-represented artists are less successful at auction than living artists or than artists affiliated with galleries that represent less popular artists. At least two potential explanations arise. First, deceased artists, who are usually already well-established if they are posthumously represented by a gallery, do not see stronger auction performance when their representing galleries allocate significant time and resources to managing other popular artists. Second, reverse causality may loom, as deceased artists with strong records at auction are more likely to be represented by single galleries run solely by their estate or galleries who are wholly loyal to honoring their legacy, creating this apparent trend of lower degree centrality corresponding to stronger auction performance.

A significant negative coefficient on the interaction between median clustering coefficient and whether the artist is Chinese more than offsets the positive coefficient on median clustering coefficient. This hints at another nuanced exception to the positive and significant relationship between median clustering coefficient and sales. Holding other variables constant, Chinese artists appear to be less likely to benefit from galleries with high clustering coefficients, implying that affiliation with galleries that lie in disparate "neighborhoods," or that have portfolios with little overlap with each other, seems to lead to greater annual sales. One hypothesis here is that, as Chinese art emerges globally, a Chinese artist who affiliates with galleries that are not tightly clustered might actually be able to tap into more niches and geographies.

Finally, of the significant indicator variables in the model, a few coefficients are especially interesting. Deceased artists perform better at auction, whereas artists under 40 perform less well. Chinese and Indian artists appear to be outselling their peers from 2013 through 2015. And tempera, prints, acrylic, and oil appear to be top-selling mediums—although a significant and negative interaction coefficient on American oil painters hints at a less bullish market for them.

The models incorporating maximum network statistics similarly see resoundingly positive and significant coefficients for their network statistics, indicating that artists affiliated with galleries with high degree centralities or that belong to gallery neighborhoods exhibiting clustering can predict success at auction. The same interaction variables (just involving maximum instead of median statistics) are significant in the same direction. Deceased artists achieve lower auction turnover as their galleries' degree centralities increase. Chinese artists with greater maximum clustering coefficients do not perform as well at auction as those with lower clustering. Interpretation of the other descriptive variables in this model echoes the first model. Deceased artists see stronger auction sales, and artists under 40 do not perform as well. Asian artists in general—especially Chinese, Turkish, and Indian artists—thrive at auction relative to their peers. Meanwhile, American artists, especially American oil painters, fare much worse. Tempera and acrylic works sell especially well.

Table 1.3 | Models for Log of Sum of Sales

	Median statistics	**Median statistics with interactions**	**Max statistics**	**Max statistics with interactions**
Median.Degree	0.001*** (0.0001)	0.003*** (0.0001)		
Median.CC	0.514*** (0.129)	0.311** (0.133)		
Max.Degree			0.002*** (0.00004)	0.002*** (0.0001)
Max.CC			2.691*** (0.080)	2.614*** (0.083)
Dead	0.936*** (0.059)	1.728*** (0.071)	0.959*** (0.052)	1.538*** (0.068)
Oil	0.526*** (0.047)	0.713*** (0.054)	0.538*** (0.042)	0.695*** (0.048)
American	-0.406*** (0.044)	-0.324*** (0.051)	-0.853*** (0.042)	-0.752*** (0.048)
Age	-0.001*** (0.0003)	-0.001** (0.0003)	-0.001*** (0.0003)	-0.001*** (0.0003)
under40	-0.438*** (0.072)	-0.373*** (0.071)	-0.416*** (0.064)	-0.408*** (0.063)
Year.of.Sales.2014	0.102** (0.040)	0.101** (0.039)	0.103*** (0.036)	0.103*** (0.035)
acrylic	0.859*** (0.079)	0.843*** (0.078)	0.681*** (0.070)	0.659*** (0.069)
tempera	1.366*** (0.504)	1.316*** (0.497)	1.327** (0.542)	1.344** (0.538)
Ink	0.344*** (0.121)	0.482*** (0.120)	0.337*** (0.107)	0.360*** (0.109)
Print	1.002*** (0.055)	0.926*** (0.055)	0.477*** (0.050)	0.448*** (0.049)
mixedmedia	0.419*** (0.102)	0.458*** (0.101)	0.319*** (0.092)	0.344*** (0.092)
drawing	0.362** (0.153)	0.290* (0.151)	0.331** (0.137)	0.274** (0.136)
Chinese	1.143*** (0.100)	1.591*** (0.175)	1.292*** (0.090)	1.841*** (0.161)
Japanese	-0.541*** (0.121)	-0.426*** (0.119)	-0.658*** (0.108)	-0.587*** (0.107)
Italian	0.312*** (0.079)	0.273*** (0.078)	0.252*** (0.071)	0.233*** (0.071)
Indian	0.904*** (0.169)	0.978*** (0.167)	0.976*** (0.152)	1.007*** (0.151)

French	0.648*** (0.076)	0.624*** (0.075)	0.587*** (0.069)	0.591*** (0.068)
Russian	0.365* (0.221)	0.402* (0.218)	0.671*** (0.198)	0.702*** (0.197)
British			-0.362*** (0.066)	-0.367*** (0.066)
Brazilian	0.578*** (0.212)	0.582*** (0.209)	0.610*** (0.178)	0.580*** (0.177)
Swedish	-0.509** (0.205)	-0.643*** (0.202)		
Turkish			1.012*** (0.283)	1.070*** (0.281)
Median.CC:Chinese		-0.866** (0.428)		
Max.CC:Chinese				-1.194*** (0.325)
Median.Degree:dead		-0.003*** (0.0002)		
Max.Degree:dead				-0.001*** (0.0001)
oil:American		-0.535*** (0.089)		-0.446*** (0.080)
Constant	9.546*** (0.068)	9.274*** (0.070)	8.053*** (0.057)	7.910*** (0.058)
Observations	13,451	13,451	13,408	13,408
R^2	0.121	0.146	0.312	0.322
Adjusted R^2	0.120	0.145	0.311	0.320

Note: Standard errors are in parentheses. *p<0.1; **p<0.05; ***p<0.01

Maximum Auction Price Models

My final models for maximum auction price (with interactions), based on median and maximum network statistics, account for 12% and 26%, respectively, of the variation in the outcome variable, the natural logarithm of an artist's most expensive work at auction in a given year. This outcome variable is closely related to the previous one but ultimately different. Maximum auction price is a measure of a single event, whereas sum of sales is a measure of all events in a given year. Both are used to discuss the financial success of artists, but this one is especially ubiquitous as a record of what an artist is capable of achieving with a single work. It is a measure of quality rather than quantity. Once again, both models corroborate my hypothesis that network statistics can serve as a new basis for analyzing artist valuations, and the log-level regression involving maximum network statistics again seems to result in less noise, with a higher coefficient of determination.

The first model based on median network statistics sees positive and significant coefficients for its network statistics, median degree centrality and median clustering coefficient. Just like for the sum of the sales model, these coefficients denote that artists affiliated with galleries that have many connections or that lie in highly clustered neighborhoods within the network are more likely to have higher records at auction. The magnitudes of the coefficients are roughly the same, as well. A unit increase in median degree centrality (just one additional connection), holding all else constant, predicts a 0.2% increase in maximum auction price.

This model includes a negative coefficient on the interaction between median degree centrality and whether the artist is deceased, implying that deceased artists do not posthumously set higher records at auction the more well-connected their galleries are. Again, deceased artists perform better at auction, while artists under 40 perform worse. Chinese, Indian, and Brazilian artists appear to be setting higher records at auction than their peers from 2013 through 2015. Tempera, prints, acrylic, and oil are top-selling mediums, and American oil painters see a significant negative coefficient here, as well. The coefficient on the interaction between median clustering coefficient and whether the artist is Chinese is negative, but it is not significant this time. However, the interaction coefficient is once again negative and significant in the maximum network statistics-based model.

The maximum network statistics regression for maximum auction price also replicates my findings in each of the other models. It presents overwhelmingly positive and significant coefficients for its network statistics (maximum degree centrality and maximum clustering coefficient) and significant and negative coefficients on the same interaction variables presented in the log of sum of sales maximum statistics model. Deceased artists do not perform better at auction with increases in their degree centrality, and Chinese artists do not appear to benefit from higher clustering coefficients among their galleries.

Fascinatingly, when I replace Chinese artists with American artists in the interaction with maximum clustering coefficient, the coefficient flips to a positive and significant one, while all other important coefficients do not change significantly. This alternative model indicates that American artists set higher records at auction when their galleries are highly clustered. This makes sense anecdotally when considering artists like Jeff Koons, whose connections to the elite and highly intertwined art circles of Gagosian, Serpentine, and Sonnabend have shaped and elevated his career. American artists like Koons may be more likely to benefit from clustering among their galleries (and the collaboration implied by these high clustering coefficients) in leading mature markets like the U.S. and U.K. than, say, Chinese artists, who see a negative interaction coefficient in the models presented earlier.

Table 1.4 | Models for Log of Maximum Auction Price

	Log of Maximum Auction Price			
	Median statistics	**Median statistics with interactions**	**Max statistics**	**Max statistics with interactions**
Median.CC	0.434*** (0.109)	0.229** (0.113)		
Median.Degree	0.001*** (0.0001)	0.002*** (0.0001)		
Max.CC			2.197*** (0.072)	2.151*** (0.077)
Max.Degree			0.002*** (0.00004)	0.002*** (0.0001)
Dead	0.670*** (0.041)	1.304*** (0.053)	0.660*** (0.038)	1.078*** (0.056)
Oil	0.443*** (0.040)	0.584*** (0.045)	0.468*** (0.038)	0.580*** (0.044)
American	-0.363*** (0.037)	-0.302*** (0.043)	-0.668*** (0.039)	-0.590*** (0.045)
Chinese	1.084*** (0.084)	1.240*** (0.149)	1.230*** (0.067)	1.608*** (0.122)
under40	-0.182*** (0.060)	-0.137** (0.060)	-0.195*** (0.059)	-0.184*** (0.059)
Year.of.Sales.2014	0.081** (0.034)	0.080** (0.034)	0.080** (0.033)	0.080** (0.033)
Acrylic	0.650*** (0.067)	0.638*** (0.066)	0.540*** (0.065)	0.525*** (0.065)
tempera	0.728* (0.438)	0.740* (0.432)	1.014*** (0.330)	1.030*** (0.329)
Ink	0.076 (0.101)	0.206** (0.101)		
Print	0.665*** (0.047)	0.603*** (0.046)	0.306*** (0.046)	0.286*** (0.046)
mixedmedia	0.180** (0.087)	0.208** (0.086)	0.128 (0.084)	0.147* (0.083)
drawing	0.526*** (0.132)	0.474*** (0.130)	0.551*** (0.114)	0.521*** (0.114)
Japanese	-0.529*** (0.102)	-0.437*** (0.101)	-0.573*** (0.094)	-0.518*** (0.094)
Italian	0.101 (0.065)	0.079 (0.065)		
Indian	0.781*** (0.144)	0.847*** (0.142)	0.861*** (0.128)	0.886*** (0.128)
French	0.265*** (0.065)	0.245*** (0.064)	0.289*** (0.064)	0.298*** (0.063)
Russian	0.385** (0.192)	0.422** (0.190)	0.624*** (0.163)	0.681*** (0.162)
German			-0.110* (0.063)	-0.109* (0.063)
British			-0.226*** (0.062)	-0.226*** (0.062)
Brazilian	0.720*** (0.180)	0.717*** (0.177)	0.666*** (0.160)	0.649*** (0.159)
Swedish	-0.538*** (0.169)	-0.641*** (0.167)		
Median.Degree:dead		-0.002*** (0.0001)		
Max.Degree:dead				-0.001*** (0.0001)
oil:American		-0.409*** (0.075)		-0.331*** (0.075)
Median.CC:Chinese		-0.103 (0.368)		

Max.CC:Chinese				-0.779*** (0.256)
Turkish			0.686*** (0.204)	0.726*** (0.204)
Constant	8.994*** (0.056)	8.800*** (0.058)	7.747*** (0.050)	7.625*** (0.052)
Observations	13,420	13,420	14,135	14,135
R^2	0.101	0.124	0.250	0.257
Adjusted R^2	0.100	0.122	0.249	0.255
Residual Std. Error	1.848 (df = 13398)	1.825 (df = 13395)	1.857 (df = 14113)	1.849 (df = 14110)
F Statistic	71.943*** (df = 21; 13398)	78.696*** (df = 24; 13395)	223.996*** (df = 21; 14113)	202.869*** (df = 24; 14110)

Note: Standard errors are in parentheses. *p<0.1; **p<0.05; ***p<0.01

Part III: IV Regressions

As an extension of my multiple regression models, I propose and set up an instrumental variable regression. I use network location shifts due to exogenous gallery closings as an instrument in hopes of establishing causality between an artist's network location and subsequent auction performance. My results are presented in Table 1.5. 18 out of 32 instrumental regressions are positive and significant at the 10% level, a promising indication that network characteristics play a causal role in artist performance at auction. However, first-stage regressions indicate that my current sample of exogenous gallery closings is still a weak instrument for the other 14 network statistics. These results can be strengthened with better network and auction data, an opportunity for future study.

Expanding this auction dataset beyond its temporal bounds of 2013 through 2015 would dramatically increase the sample of exogenous network location shifts to study. For example, gallery closings in 2012 due to Hurricane Sandy in New York were a random shock to the network that displaced many artists. 2012, however, is just outside the scope of this dataset. Chronological data on the networks side would also improve the viability of this instrument. Instead of generating a hypothetical network and recalculating network statistics after a gallery is removed from the network, as I do in this paper, network data with a time dimension would more accurately represent the post-shock network. Nonetheless, in over 50% of our models, this instrument demonstrates that gallery networks play a causal role in an artist's valuation at auction.

Table 1.5 | IV Regression Output

	Log of Sum of Sales	*Log of Maximum Auction Price*
Median Degree	0.031 (0.037)	0.027 (0.032)
Max Degree	0.005*** (0.002)	0.004*** (0.001)
Median Weighted Degree	-0.009 (0.014)	-0.008 (0.012)
Max Weighted Degree	0.001*** (0.0004)	0.001*** (0.0004)
Median Closeness	53.049* (32.01)	45.459* (27.499)
Max Closeness	25.946** (10.297)	22.233** (8.877)
Median Betweenness	-1432.247 (2062.971)	-1227.324 (1763.764)
Max Betweenness	210.254*** (81.305)	180.171** (70.363)
Median PageRank	-7612.13 (13651.72)	-6523.002 (11680.2)
Max PageRank	873.925*** (323.507)	748.886*** (280.342)
Median Eigenvector	25.245 (22.601)	21.633 (19.437)
Max Eigenvector	5.465*** (1.933)	4.683*** (1.676)
Median Clustering Coefficient	-98.103 (211.133)	-84.067 (180.905)
Max Clustering Coefficient	8.870*** (3.399)	7.601*** (2.935)
Median Weighted CC	-365.825 (2904.727)	-313.483 (2488.631)
Max Weighted CC	9.918*** (3.831)	8.499** (3.309)

Note: Standard errors are in parentheses. Each coefficient in this table corresponds to a single IV regression. "CC" is an abbreviation for clustering coefficient. Note that 18 out of 32 hypothesis tests yield significant and positive results. *p<0.1; **p<0.05; ***p<0.01

6. Discussions & Limitations

My results across three sets of analyses—hypothesis testing, multiple regression, and IV regressions—indicate that network statistics serve as excellent predictors of an artist's success at auction. In 29 out of 32 hypothesis tests, I find significant evidence to reject the null hypothesis that network statistics are not significantly and positively correlated with success at auction. Across my two sets of models (sum of sales and maximum hammer prices), I find that network statistics are meaningful contributors to valuation prediction; these models account for as much as 32% of the variation in response data (R^2). Lastly, this paper points to potential causality, though imperfectly so: 18 out of 32 instrumental regressions indicate that network characteristics play a causal role in an artist's financial performance.

Four potential limitations related to my dataset and methodological assumptions are worth noting in conjunction with my conclusions.

Non-random sampling in Artsy dataset: While Artsy's dataset may be the biggest one available, it is not the population nor a random sample of the art world's institutions and artists. The artists represented lean modern and contemporary, and the artists and their representing institutions have all seen some success at auction already, as Artsy's clients tend to be higher tier institutions. Additionally, the network statistics I run are, to a certain extent, dependent on the number of works and artists the institution has uploaded to Artsy. A partner institution that is important in the real art world network might not appear important in my results if its catalog of artists on Artsy is not complete or representative.

Selection bias and data omission in Artnet dataset: The Artnet dataset, while the most comprehensive available, still leaves out the majority of artists in the Artsy network dataset given that the data covers only the past three years, and only for artists who sold work at reputable auction houses. In other words, the sample in this study is heavily biased toward the auction performance of the Olympians of the art world, instead of all its constituents, introducing sample selection bias. Data omission is a related potential concern. While the Artsy dataset consists of over 27,000 artists, the study's final models ultimately only include 14,140 observations for 6,090 artists. A more comprehensive auction performance dataset might lend greater external validity to my models.

Human error: Given that many of the artist's names in this study were manually adjusted to allow for a more accurate and comprehensive join between the network and auction dataset, human error could have led to some mismatching or accidental omission of data. Multiple accepted spellings of many artists' names further compounded the risk of mismatching—for example, Chiu Ya-Tsai, Chiu Yatsai, and Qiu Yacai are three accepted spellings of the same name.

Omitted variable bias and reverse causality: While my proposed instrument promisingly suggests a direction of causation, omitted variable bias and reverse causality remain potential limitations. For example, increases in an artist's auction revenue may drive more galleries to seek to represent that artist, and these kinds of galleries may be more likely to exhibit certain network behavior like clustering or high closeness centrality. More research disentangling network importance, auction performance, and their effects on each other is needed.

7. Extensions

In light of the regression results and the limitations outlined in the previous section, I suggest the following extensions to further test my hypotheses.

Increasing the size and diversity of the instrument's sample: This paper suggests that further studies expand the dataset of artists whose galleries shut down exogenously by strengthening both the network and auction datasets. Greater diversity in the galleries included should also be prioritized. Currently, the gallery closings that form the sample in this paper's IV regression are prominent gallery shutdowns featured in news outlets, mostly affecting artists who have already established enough provenance to fare well at auction regardless of network location. For example, Yvon Lambert's collection of artists (Sol LeWitt, On Kawara, Keith Haring, Louise Lawler, etc.) are highly successful artists who have already accumulated enough credibility and acclaim to withstand sudden shifts in their network location. I hypothesize that artists in earlier stages of their careers, for whom gallery representation is still an essential part of their development, would see more volatile changes in their auction performance after exogenous shifts in their network geography.

Further network segmentation by artist nationality, medium, age: Connectivity and network statistics could vary widely between artists of different ages, nationalities, and mediums. Rather than look at the gallery network as a whole, one might gain more insight by studying all the networks within the greater global gallery network more closely. Future papers might look specifically at one sociological network, such as Japanese galleries or the market for Western oil paintings.

Outside of art: Finally, it is worth briefly mentioning that additional work at the intersection of network theory and the art market can further public understanding of networks within other fields. Network tools might be able to unpack phenomena in numerous other bipartite markets: professors switching between a small number of universities that bid up their wages, private wealth advisors on Wall Street jumping between firms to negotiate more favorable commissions and performance fees, sports teams and top players, etc. These potential extensions all motivate continued study and application of network ideas to the art world.

8. Conclusion

This study is among the first to bring network analyses to art valuation discussions at scale. By constructing a monopartite network of galleries connected by shared artists via their portfolios, calculating network statistics, conducting hypothesis tests, and constructing robust models for auction performance based on these network characteristics, this study finds that network characteristics have significant and positive correlations with auction performance, as measured by auction turnover and top hammer price. Additionally, shifts in network location due to sudden and exogenous gallery closings present a promising avenue toward understanding how network importance might causally influence auction performance. Suggested next steps include expanding the IV regression sample size and further segmentation of the global gallery network. This study takes a robust first step toward understanding how networks within the art world affect the nodes, agents, and institutions that inhabit it, concluding that gallery affiliations are indeed critical predictors of performance at auction. Though true artistic genius should not be overlooked, this study finds that an artwork's price is determined by much more than an artwork's intrinsic qualities.

9. Acknowledgements

This paper would not have been possible without the generosity of Artsy and the guidance of my colleagues Richard B. Freeman and Sophie Qingzhen Wang. I would also like to acknowledge Benjamin Golub, Dale Jorgenson, and Scott Kominers of the Harvard Economics Department; Heather Inwood of the University of Cambridge Faculty of Asian and Middle Eastern Studies, Matt Saunders of the Harvard Visual and Environmental Studies Department; Gizem Saka of the Wharton School of Business; Jessica Backus of Artsy; and Shalimar Fojas White and Jessica Evans Brady of the Harvard Fine Arts Library for their contributions to the conception and development of this research topic, which initially began in 2016 as an undergraduate dissertation for the Harvard Economics Department. I thank them for their continued time and insight.

10. Appendix

Figure 1.A.1 | Visualization of Monopartite Gallery Network

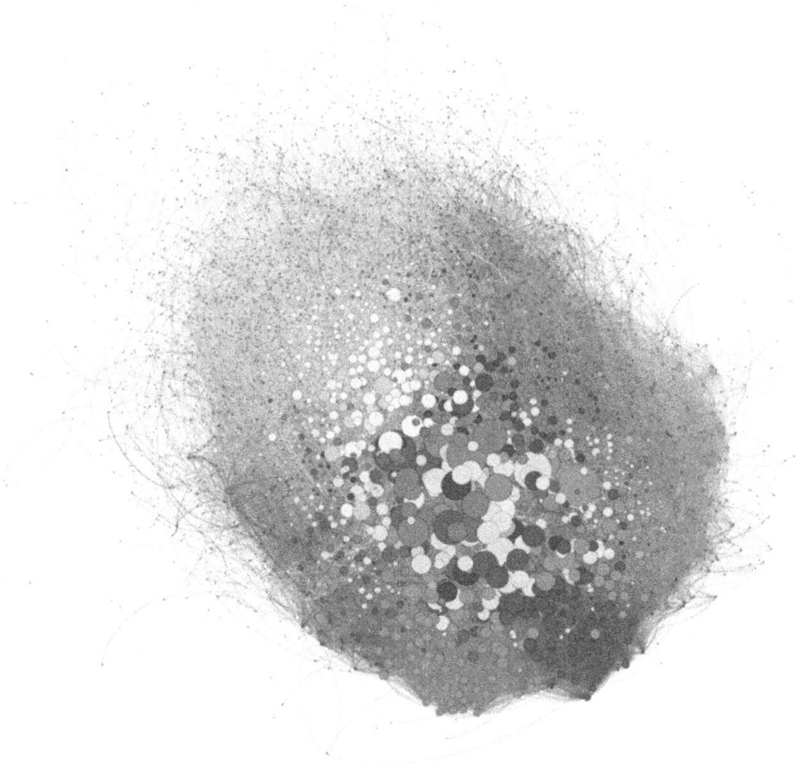

Note: Node size based on degree count, colored by modularity.

11. References

Amaral, Luis A. N. 2000. "Classes of Small-World Networks." *Proceedings of the National Academy of Sciences of the United States of America* 97, no. 21: pp. 11149-11152. [doi: 10.1073/pnas.200327197]

Andrea Rosen Gallery. "Felix Gonzalez-Torres." Andrea Rosen Gallery. (Accessed: May 23, 2020). http://www.andrearosengallery.com/archived-gallery-site-1990-2017

Artsy. "About | Artsy." Artsy. (Accessed: March 9, 2017). artsy.net/about

Barber, Lynn. "Bleeding art." The Guardian. (Accessed: April 19, 2003). theguardian.com/artanddesign/2003/apr/20/thesaatchigallery.art6

Barrat, Alain, et al. 2004. "The Architecture of Complex Weighted Networks." *Proceedings of the National Academy of Sciences* 101, no. 11: 3747-3752. [doi: 10.1073/pnas.0400087101]

Braden, Laura E. A. 2018. "Networks Created Within Exhibition: The Curators' Effect on Historical Recognition." *American Behavioral Scientist* 63: pp. 01-19. [doi: 10.1177/0002764218800145]

Campos, Nauro F., and Renata L. Barbosa. 2009. "Paintings and Numbers: An Econometric Investigation of Sales Rates, Prices, and Returns in Latin American Art Auctions." *Oxford Economic Papers* 61, no. 1: pp. 28–51.

Etro, Federico, and Elena Stepanova. 2018. "Power-laws in art." *Physica A* 506: pp. 217-220. [doi: 10.1016/j.physa.2018.04.057]

Giuffre, Katherine. 1999. "Sandpiles of Opportunity: Success in the Art World." *Social Forces* 77, no. 3: pp. 815-832. [doi: 10.2307/3005962]

Kazakina, Katya. "Art Flippers Chase Fresh Stars as Murillo's Doodles Soar." Bloomberg. (Accessed: February 7, 2014). bloomberg.com/news/2014-02-06/art-flippers-chase-fresh-stars-as-murillo-s-doodles-soar.html

Kennedy, Maev. "Art market 'a cultural obscenity'." *The Guardian.* (Accessed: June 3, 2004). theguardian.com/uk/2004/jun/03/arts.artsnews

Kinsella, Eileen. "What Does TEFAF 2016 Art Market Report Tell Us About The Global Art Trade?" *Artnet News.* (Accessed: March 10, 2016). news.artnet.com/market/tefaf-2016-art-market-report-443615

Kogut, Bruce, and Gordon Walker. 2001. "The Small World of Germany and the Durability of National Networks." *American Sociological Review* 66, no. 3: pp. 317-335. [doi: 10.2307/3088882]

Pearson Prentice. "Advanced Diagnostics for Multiple Regression: A Supplement to Multivariate Data Analysis." Mvstats. (Accessed: May 23, 2020). mvstats.com/downloads/supplements/advanced_regression_diagnostics.pdf

Rengers, Merijn, and Olav Velthuis. 2002. "Determinants of Prices for Contemporary Art in Dutch Galleries, 1992-1998." *Journal of Cultural Economics* 26, no.1: pp. 01-28.

Schönfeld, Susanne, and Andreas Reinstaller. 2007. "The Effects of Gallery and Artist Reputation on Prices in the Primary Market for Art: A Note." *Journal of Cultural Economics* 31, no. 2: pp. 143–153.

Stuckism International Gallery. "A Dead Shark Isn't Art." Stuckism International Gallery. (Accessed: May 22, 2020). stuckism.com/Shark.html

Thompson, Donald N. 2012. *The $12 Million Stuffed Shark: The Curious Economics of Contemporary Art and Auction Houses.* London: Aurum.

Uzzi, Brian, and Jarret Spiro. 2005. "Collaboration and Creativity: The Small World Problem." *American Journal of Sociology* 111, no. 2: pp. 447-504. [doi: 10.1086/432782]

Wang, Annie. "Sotheby's Opens London Private Sales Gallery with Beuys." Art in America / Art News. (Accessed: September 4, 2013). artnews.com/art-in-america/features/sothebys-opens-london-private-sales-gallery-with-beuys-58839/

Zorloni, Alessia. 2005. "Structure of the Contemporary Art Market and the Profile of Italian Artists." *International Journal of Arts Management* 8, no. 1: pp. 61-71.

Chapter 2

How Neoliberalism Shapes Contemporary Art Market: *Structure, Assessment, and Scope*

Marek Prokůpek, Ph.D.

University of Economics, Prague, Czech Republic

Abstract

Neoliberalism has framed art in purely financial terms and shifted the focus to its economic contribution rather than an appreciation of art for art's sake. This economization of art has increasingly exposed artists and institutions to a market power and toward the adoption of a more commercial and business-oriented approach. The impact of neoliberalism on the non-profit art sector is connected to the privatization and deregulation of traditionally state-subsidized organizations and the perception as an engine for economic development. The latter captured by economic impact studies. In this chapter, the impact of neoliberalism is explored at several levels from the transformation of business models of art market players, through the rising power of financial institutions, and the branding to expand valuation. All aspects are associated with an increased view of art as an investment asset. The desire to satisfy such demand for the valuation standardization of artworks has been fulfilled by price indices based on auction sales and artists' rankings. These tendencies prove that the concept of art for art's sake has weakened and the acknowledgement and recognition of quality streams from the market success of the artist. Traditionally, the non-transparent art market, characterized by the asymmetry of information, has required more precise data. Numerous reports on the art market are published annually and provide information on the current trends and tendencies. The art market has been, therefore, challenged and shifted by the apparent neoliberal ideology in the direction of marketization and monetization.

Keywords: Art index; art market; economization of art; neoliberalism; value of art.

* * *

1. Introduction

The art market is almost as old as art itself, and similarly, as art, the art market has undergone significant changes over time. It has adjusted to social, political, economic, and technological changes. Neoliberalism, which refers to the exceptional renaissance of doctrines of the free market (Gamble 2001), has brought several challenges to the traditional art market players and caused structural changes.

McGuigan defines neoliberalism as "the return to a once discredited liberalism in political economy, the nineteenth-century espousal of laisse-faire economics for free trade in an international division of labor and minimal state intervention within the nation" (McGuigan 2005, 230). He argues that the idea of the free play of market forces that have never been free is vulnerable to repetitive crises and enhances inequality.

The neoliberalism of the arts and culture that tends to frame them in purely financial terms has shifted focus to their economic contribution and enhanced corporate engagement in arts and culture, mainly through philanthropy giving, sponsorship, public-private partnership, or art collecting. Consequently, artists and professionals involved in the art world and art organizations have adopted a more commercial and business-oriented approach (Alexander 2018). Business models of art organizations have changed and adjusted to the economic, social, political, and technical changes and developed entrepreneurial spirit strategies (Carbonare and Prokůpek 2020). Emphasis has been placed on measurable indicators of success, and subjects in the art world have aimed to outperform their main competitors (Chong 2009). Another significant consequence of neoliberalist tendencies is that art has been increasingly seen as an investment asset (Moreau et al. 2015).

The global art market has been with acceleration penetrated by the neoliberal practices, which has consequently changed approaches to more-market oriented assessment and valuations methods and consumption practices in the art markets represented by art indices, databases, reports, and online applications.

Another aspect of the neoliberal powers imposed on the art world is the diminishment of the strict distinction between the public and private art sectors. This trend can be illustrated by the example of a trend when individual art dealers and superstar auction houses sponsor exhibitions in public art museums.

The main question framing this chapter is: How neoliberal tendencies have impacted the art market? We can see shifts in business models of traditional art mediators and the penetration of new actors such as financial institutions playing the role of collectors, financial providers and advisors. This has also imposed the shift of the interactions between these players.

2. Concept of the Art Market

The art market is a space where art interconnects with money and collecting with investing. Thanks to the art market's existence, one can obtain works that one wants to own, and at a price that reflects both supply and demand in the market. The art market is one of the forms of business in culture and art and refers to the trade in works of art, in which their property rights change.

Magnus Resch (2015) describes the art market as a mechanism of collecting, purchasing, and selling artworks. In other words, it represents a distribution system that makes art accessible as a commodity and gives it a particular value. The artwork is a specific type of commodity since it is a result of individual creative work produced by an artist. Thus it is a highly unique and heterogenous product with minimal supply and without substitutes.

On the other hand, Iain Robertson (2005) emphasizes the informational value of an artwork, because according to him, every work is valued mainly for its idea. James Goodwin (2008) sees the art market as a mechanism that can assign a monetary value to the intangible value of art. His view is based on Smith's theory of the market from the end of the 18th century, which was developed by David Ricardo in the 19th century. Mainly the principle of innovation is vital for the art market. Ricardo claimed that the competition encourages innovation and differentiation of products, which is in the art market reflected by the evolution of artistic creation. Goodwin (2008) also emphasizes the aesthetic perception of the market and its relation between monetary value and its impact on society. He considers the evolution of the art market the same as any other market with a specific product.

Resch (2015) points out that the art market, unlike the financial market, is inefficient. It lacks transparency, it is difficult for buyers to obtain relevant information, and the art market structure is very fluid. To be successful in the art market requires a high level of personal involvement and effort in the process of information gathering. Though most markets are based on the exchange of information that establishes prices, the art market usually provides data only to stakeholders. Publicly available information is only the result of the auction market. Therefore, there is a lack of data about sales in galleries and via other dealers.

Resch (2015) also claims that the art market is less liquid than other markets. Artworks have a subjective value for their owners, and their economic value (price) is volatile and fluctuates over time. Thus, people are reluctant to buy and sell works of art as often as financial assets. Another factor of low liquidity is the relatively long-time gap (even several months or years) between selling the work and the actual sale. Michael Reid (2004) takes the opposite view from Magnus Resch and advises investors to diversify their portfolio by purchasing works of art. Reid explains that although the artwork is an investment and asset, the correlation between the art market and stocks is tiny. If the value of shares falls, the amount of bonds (and other financial assets) usually decreases, but the value of works of art is stagnating (or decreasing vary slightly compared to a fall in the price of bonds).

Last but not least, the art market is characterized by its distortions. A typical example is auction sales, in which the price is deliberately pushed as high as possible. Record sales are attractive to journalists, raise the rates of other works by the same author, and allow all different starting prices to be raised during subsequent auctions. Another example of market disruption is insider trading, which is a desirable and welcome source of profit in the art market. The prices of the works depend on the social links between the seller and the buyer—a famous and acclaimed collector will never have the same selling price as his young colleague.

The term art market refers to the commerce in art objects that engage change in ownership and includes auction houses, commercial galleries, and other actors involved in the buying and selling artwork. This definition characterizes the art market from broader terms art business and art world. The art business refers to all activities surrounding the production, commerce, and exhibition. Moreover, the term art business also covers all people who are somehow professionally involved in the art business. It includes both commercial and non-commercial subject. The even broader term the art world consists of every activity and venue where art is presented, including museums, commercial and non-commercial art galleries, art schools and schools where art history is taught, and publications dedicated to art and other places (Taylor 2017).

The art market is generally distinguished into the primary and secondary art markets. The primary art market refers to artworks being sold for the first time and often works as a synonym for contemporary art. On the other hand, the secondary market deals with artworks that have been previously sold at least once and often function as a synonym for a market with old masters. Traditionally, different art market players worked either at the primary art market or the secondary art market, and some do both. In the last two decades, the role and intersections of such players have changed. For example, auction houses, traditionally a dominant actor of the secondary market, started to penetrate the primary market.

The traditional art market was usually dominated by a small group of actors, including collectors or patrons, rather than a massive number of mediators. Gradually the concept of "art for art's sake" has diminished, and commodification and financialization started to play essential roles in art markets (Lee 2018). Art has been created for a variety of purposes over time, including religious and secular, or as a statement of power. In the last two decades, art has witnessed increasing marketization (Joy and Sherry Jr 2003; Lee 2018).

The art market offers opportunities for many players. These players have evolved with time and have different roles. Generally, we can divide art market players into two pillars. The artists represent one pillar and collectors the other one, all players between these two pillars are intermediaries, and they can be divided into commercial or conceptual art mediators. Resch (2015) creates a scheme of the art market players based on the distinction between the primary and secondary art market and conceptual and commercial art mediators. Conceptual art mediators are represented by critics and museums. Their role is much more influential on the primary art market than the secondary art market since they can be more influential on the career of young emerging artists than old masters already proved by the market. Objects exhibited in art museums are generally considered as of high quality. Therefore museums have reliable power over the position of artists on the market. On the side of commercial art, mediators are art gallery dealers, private art dealers, auction houses, and ancillary art business providers. Art galleries usually do both, primary and secondary art market, auction houses have been traditionally more influential on the secondary art market, but it has changed in the last decade.

3. Neoliberalisation of the Art Market

The neoliberalisation of the art world is connected to the economization of the art. In the 1980s, arts and culture started to be perceived as a tool for socio-economic development. Myerscough's report The Economic Importance of the Arts in Britain (1988) capturing art as an essential driver of employment, wealth, and tourism. Eräranta, Moisander, and Penttilä (2019, 20) argue that

> the ongoing economization of the arts is currently driven by the various national and local governments and transnational organizations, such as the European Union and the Organization for Economic Co-operation and Development, seeking to leverage art for socio-economic development and various other biopolitical purposes. In doing so, they

> operate as active participants – if not the key players – in those discursive and non-discursive practices and processes through which the economic logic of the market is extended to the domain of arts and cultural institutions.

The tendency to perceive art as an engine for socio-economic development has created a trend of economic impact studies widely used in the arts and cultural sectors in the last three decades. These studies aim to prove that the existence of an art organization or art event has a significant contribution to the local or national economy. This is most probably true, but with this optics comes the tendency to value art based on its economic contribution. Many cities have tended to follow the commercial success of the Guggenheim museum in Bilbao, framed by the term Bilbao effect. These impulses, connected to the neoliberal marketization of the art, can be observed not only in the non-commercial art sector. Art fairs have become a tool to enhance the image of a city or region. Art Basel, the event considered one of the most important art fairs in the art world, has expanded to Miami and Hong Kong.

Several scholars have pointed out that marketization in the field of art springs from practices of neoliberal governance that puts pressure on artists and arts organizations to consider themselves as market-oriented businesses (Alexander 2018; Alexander and Bowler 2014; Eräranta et al. 2019), which naturally influences the way art is valued and what role it plays in the society. Eräranta et al. (2019) argue that in neoliberal capitalism, art seems to be redefined in economic terms, and the market has become the central arbiter of truth in the art world.

Neoliberalism has enhanced globalization. McGuigan defines neo-liberal globalization as "the revival of free-market economic policy and its rapid diffusion around the world with enormous social-structural and cultural consequences" (McGuigan 2005, 230). Art fairs represent a significant symbol of globalization of the art and the most commercial aspect of the art market. Art fairs are a place where supply and demand meet. They represent an opportunity for galleries and dealers to extend their customer base and collectors to see the current trends in the art world. Art fairs are becoming more and more important players. According to the Art Basel and UBS Report, art fairs are a critical part of the art market's infrastructure, providing a large portion of the art market's sales. Fairs have become central to many dealers' business models and continue to be a vital force gathering dealers and their buyers together from all parts of the world. The boom of art fairs is rapid; in 2000, there were around 55 established international art fairs. In 2019 this number expanded to 300 international art fairs with hundreds of regional and local fairs (McGuigan 2005).

In 2019, the art market witnessed several new fairs, particularly in Asia, including Taipei Dangdai, S.E.A. Focus in Singapore, Art Moments Jakarta, and Nanjing International Art Fair. The Western art world significantly dominates the contemporary art market (Buchholz and Wuggenig 2005; Quemin 2006). Over the last two decades, the Asian art market has started to play a more critical role (Velthuis and Baia Curioni 2016; Lee 2018). The Chicago Invitational and Frieze Los Angeles also opened in the US in 2019. The significance of the art fairs is proved by the increasing value of sales. The share of dealers' annual sales by value made at art fairs grew from less than 30% in 2010 to 45% in 2019. This is close to parity with purchases made through galleries, which increased 2% year-on-year to 50% but have declined steadily over the last decade as the event-driven marketplace has continued to capture an increasing share of sales through fairs. Many galleries have noted that newer collectors were now more aware of and loyal to fairs than their individual exhibiting galleries, as these events have become the new global focus for sales. While not everyone viewed this positively, most agreed that this presented them with more significant opportunities to meet new clients who were not previously aware of their galleries or programs (McGuigan 2005, 193).

As art fairs have become crucial aspects of most art galleries' business models, the costs of participation in established international art fairs have significantly increased. This influences the content of art fair exhibitions. According to the Art Basel and UBS Report, including results of the survey among dealers, the rising costs and competitiveness of art fairs forces participating dealers to show a narrower selection of more commercial works to ensure they can sell them and cover expenses. This trend, therefore, again increases inequality, leads towards the promotion of a group of specific, commercial, and established artists thus reduces diversity:

> Although the issue of a collector (and gallery) 'fair fatigue' has been talked about for several years, many dealers also noted that some of their artists were also feeling increasingly pressured and drained by the urgency to produce new works for fairs. Some thought that the limited exhibition space and context meant that some artists were forced to make smaller and more saleable works than they might have made for a gallery or museum show. To the extent that art fair exhibitions crowded these out, this could have a significant impact on the content of works created by several sought-after artists. (McAndrew 2020, 219)

The impact of neoliberalism in the non-profit art sector is illustrated mainly by the privatization and deregulation of traditionally state-funded organizations. They have been exposed to the market powers and have been pressured to become more entrepreneurial. As the term indicates, the subject in the art market has always been exposed to the market. Karin M. Ekström (2019, 1) points out that:

> Market ideologies based on ideas of a market economy are present in sectors of society that traditionally have not been seen as markets such as education, health care, and culture although the degree of market orientation is emphasized to a different extent. In many different spheres of society, citizens are no longer merely thought of as consumers, but they are now considered customers. Ideas of a market economy have changed the role of the state versus the role of the private market in the cultural sector during the last decades. There is an increasing number of private museums and state-funded museums that are expected to operate in a market-oriented manner.

4. Business Models Transformation

Art market players have been forced to restructure their business models to make them more sustainable for the current economic and social climate that they form at the same time. With the increasing globalization, players extend their art business beyond their countries' borders and activate new online strategies.

Auction houses, traditionally a strong player on the secondary market, have changed their role and have penetrated the primary art market and the sphere of contemporary art. The milestone in the development was a two-day auction sale Beautiful Inside My Head Forever, including artworks only by Damien Hirst. The auction took place at Sotheby's London in 2008 on the same day as the collapse of Lehman Brothers (Chong 2019). This step from the auction house and the artists, who bypassed his dealer, set a precedent that auction houses sell contemporary artworks that have not been sold before.

The vital innovation present in the business models of many dealers is online selling. A higher number of artworks can be seen on websites or private art galleries or auction houses than in person. This trend can save money to art market players and allow them to reach potential buyers worldwide. Art online sales can also be a considerable threat to the art market mediators as it provides an opportunity for artists to bypass their dealers and sell directly to the consumers (Belk 2019).

5. The Rising Power of Financial Institutions

In the last three decades, the art market has been penetrated by many new players. One of them is financial institutions such as banks, insurance companies, and investment funds. Lee (2018, p. 69) says: "The influx of money into art markets through financial institutions brought a broad shift in how capital is intermediated, from artistic institutions to financial institutions" and he also argues that the financialization of art worlds involves the changeover from financial to cultural capital in the form of buying art with money and from cultural to financial capital such as charging 0% interest rate for the art loan to VIP collectors in auction houses (Lee 2018). Financial institutions have different roles in the art market. First of all, they represent the side of demand through their art collections. Companies such as Deutsche Bank, JP Morgan, UBS, and others have been systematically collecting contemporary art for investment, marketing, and PR, to enhance relationships with their employees or because of the philanthropic approach of CEOs of such companies. Objects belonging to corporate art collections are often exhibited in lobbies or offices and, in some cases, are lent to art exhibitions in museums and exhibition spaces. The boom of corporate art collections has led to the development of private art museums. Private are museums are not usually founded by financial institutions, but the ones operating in the sector of creative industries or by their CEOs, especially fashion, among others Louis Vuitton Foundation in Paris or Prada Foundation in Milan.

The second role of financial institutions in the art market comes with developing their art advisory departments. In this case, banks provide art advising services to their clients, so-called art experts recommend clients what artworks should be purchased, what artist is worth investment, and who will possibly increase their status as art connoisseurs. Some banks and other institutions also offer advice on how to build and take care of art collections. These advisory services use one of the art market's economic characteristics: the asymmetry of information. The information character of artistic goods entails difficulty evaluating the quality of the object, especially for those who do not have historical-artistic skills. This creates an asymmetry of information between buyers and sellers (Zorloni 2013). The third role of financial institutions in the art market is the role of sponsors or philanthropists. First of all, companies are often sponsors of museums or other art venues and events, including non-commercial art exhibitions and commercial art fairs. Moreover, they provide awards and prices for young, emerging artists.

Since the 2000s, the art world has experienced an increasing number of art funds. The aim of art funds is a pure investment. Investors provide money, and managers of funds offer investment portfolios. Horowitz (2014, 256) points out that "a few topics in the art market have been as energetically discussed yet as poorly understood as investing." He sees the reason behind that in its controversial nature. This practice has a pejorative meaning by many artists and a significant part of the art world. It is considered a bankrupt of the art and a loss of spiritual value, and it is perceived as a severe penetration and enhancement of capitalism into the culture. The art funds enable participation in the art market to more people who would not invest in artworks without the expertise provided by fund managers. Funds also claim that they bring liquidity and transparency to a market (Horowitz 2014). Lee (2018) sees that the boom of art funds enhances the concept of art investment, and he identifies three main reasons why art has become an attractive asset. First, it has low costs of maintenance. Second, art funds do not usually focus on a specific kind of fine arts, unlike many collections or galleries. Third, financial markets can provide better purchasing power than a gallery.

6. Marketization

Lee (2018) describes the marketization of the art world in two aspects: commodification and financialization. He continues that the commodification of the modern and contemporary art world happened not through mass production but through standardization that is against the traditional valuation of art.

The critique of the commodification of artworks is connected to critical theorists Theodor Adorno and Max Horkheimer, who brought the term cultural industry in the discussion. This term, together with creative industries, is nowadays primarily associated with the economic value of cultural and creative industries. But Adorno and Horkheimer brought this term with a pejorative connotation in the chapter "The Culture Industry: Enlightenment as Mass Deception" of the book Dialectic of Enlightenment published in 1947 (Adorno and Horkheimer 1947). In this chapter, they compare popular culture to a factory producing standardized cultural goods used to manipulate mass society into passivity. The terms factory and art would traditionally not be associated. Still, Andy Warhol called his studio the factory, where he produced a series of silkscreened copies of consumer goods packages, celebrity photographs, and dollar signs (Belk 2019).

Nowadays, we can see even more direct relationship between art and mass production. Contemporary artists, to be more precise—the famous contemporary artists, cooperate with fashion brands. Tracey Emin designing a bag for Longchamp, Richard Prince and Marc Jacobs creating together the spring/summer 2008 Louis Vuitton collection, Alexander McQueen cooperating with Damien Hirst and creating iconic skull print scarf, or Takashi Murakami designing bags for Louis Vuitton, these are just a few examples of contemporary artists engaging with mass production.

7. Towards Standardization of Valuation

"The neo-liberal marketization of art worlds has focused on the standardized valuation of artworks to facilitate trading" (Lee 2018, p. 70). The valuation of artwork is a complex and demanding process—including judgments—from an expert, consumers, market mediators, and idiosyncratic producers (Velthuis and Baia Curioni 2016; Lee 2018). In the traditional art market, prices were usually hidden to people not involved in purchasing and selling artworks; therefore, art was seen less as an investment opportunity and more as art for art's sake.

Recently, several valuation methods have appeared to assign a monetary value to artworks and assess their investment potential. The art world has witnessed the boom of several ranking such as top contemporary artworks sold at auctions, top most collected artists, most visited art fairs, most visited museums, etc. Numbers have become crucial in assessing and valuing artworks, artists, and other art market players.

With the increasing trend of considering artworks as investment assets, there has been a boom in the development of art indices. Several scholars have created an art price index based on the auction sales data. Goetzmann (1993) developed an index that allows the comparison of painting price movements to stock-market fluctuations and also an evaluation of the risk and return characteristics of art investment. Pesando (1993) builds his study on the repeat sales of modern prints at auction for 1977-1992. Chanel (1995) focused on his research on the relationship between art and the financial market. His results indicate that financial markets influence the art market with a lag of about one year. Art market behavior was also observed by Gérard-Varet (1995). Candela and Scorcu (1997) proposed a price index for modern and contemporary paintings based on estimates and auction prices. Four years later, they published a paper where they developed price indices for the secondary market for prints and drawings in Italy for 1977-1999 (Candela and Scorcu 2001). Mei and Moses (2005) determined the change in the value of art objects over the various holding periods. Higgs and Worthington (2005) focused their study on financial returns and price determinants in the Australian art market using auction sales data from the period 1973-2003. Kraeussl and Logher (2010) analyzed art markets in Russia, China, and India. Renneboog and Spaenjers (2013) investigated the price determinants and investment performance of art by applying a hedonic regression analysis to a data set of more than one million auction transactions of paintings and works on paper. David, Oosterlinck, and Szafarz (2013) use a sizeable auction-based index to claim that the art market is inefficient, mainly because price formation is opaque to outsiders who lack information on unsold artworks.

Lee (2018, 71) points out

> The commodification of artworks and artists as a part of neoliberal marketization invites three different types of commensurations, which have one clear goal, that is, to quantify the value of the artwork and the intangible characteristics of artists to assist collectors in comparing among alternatives and making their investment decisions.

The accuracy of such art indices is questionable. They are calculated based only on auction sales since these are only publicly available data on the art market sales. Nevertheless, these indices, in particular Mei Moses' Art Index, is widely used by art dealers, galleries, art funds in order not only to attract potential investors but also to produce a guideline for art funds and derivatives based on the index (Lee 2018).

8. Expansion of Markets and Brands

Neoliberalism has caused not only rapid market expansion worldwide but also a massive development of branding. Neoliberalism promotes the language of branding in all aspects of our life, including the art market (McGuigan 2005, 233). Big superstar galleries such as White Cube, Gagosian, Hauser & Wirth, Perrotin, and others have expanded and opened their branches in other continents and focus their activities on the Asian market. This trend has not touched only commercial art market mediators, but also conceptual ones. Mainly superstar museums, a term invented by Frey (1998), witnessed the demand for their brands. The Guggenheim's Foundation with its former director Thomas Krens was a pioneer in this trend, sometimes called museum franchising. The successful case of Guggenheim Bilbao, the result of negotiation between Krens and Bilbao, has been well documented, particularly its positive economic impact (Plaza 2006), which has the ambition to become a blueprint for similar projects. Bilbao was a specific case hardly repeatable in other parts of the globe. Other museums have followed this trend and sold their brands. Therefore we can visit Louvre in Abu Dhabí, Centre Pompidou in Shanghai, and others. This trend has also raised fierce criticism, including the pejorative term Mcdonaldisation of art.

According to Rifkin (2000), cultural production has diminished physical production in world trade, and he calls this concept "cultural capitalism." That means that the culture is becoming fully commercialized, and the Internet plays a crucial tool in the commercialization of the culture.

9. Conclusion

This chapter discusses the impact of neoliberalism on the art market, structure, assessment, and scope. During the last three decades, the art market has undergone significant changes, and traditional players have faced extraordinary challenges. Increasing globalization has led to the expansion of superstar galleries and art fairs, enhancing the idea of the escalating importance of brands in the art world. The art market has also been penetrated by new players, such as financial institutions that have occupied several roles on both demand and supply sides. The tendencies to consider artworks as an investment asset has led to the demand for the standardization of valuation methods. Therefore, several art price indices have been created and widely applied using auction sales data. Such indices have been used by financial institutions, art dealers, consulting companies, and art funds to represent genuine investment interests in purchasing artwork. These tendencies prove that the concept of art for art's sake has been diminishing, and the stamp of quality of artwork streams from a market success of an artist. Thus, every year, several ranking of contemporary artists are created. Traditionally not transparent art market characterized by the asymmetry of information has required more and precise data. Numbers of reports on the art market are published annually, providing information about current trends and tendencies. The art market has been therefore challenged and shifted by the apparent neoliberal ideology toward marketization and financialization.

References

Adorno, Theodor, and Max Horkheimer. 1947. *Dialectic of Enlightenment*. New York: Herder and Herder.

Alexander, Victoria D. 2018. "Enterprise Culture and the Arts: Neoliberal Values and British Art Institutions'." In *Art and the Challenge of Markets Volume 1*, edited by Victoria D. Alexander et al. Cham: Palgrave McMillan.

Alexander, Victoria D., and Anne E. Bowler. 2014. "Art at the Crossroads: The Arts in Society and the Sociology of Art." *Poetics* 43: pp. 01-19. [https://doi.org/10.1016/j.poetic.2014.02.003]

Belk, Rusell. 2019. "High-End Contemporary Art: Art for art's sake or art for mart's sake?" In *Museum Marketization: Cultural Institutions in the Neoliberal Era*, edited by Karin. M. Ekström. New York: Routledge.

Buchholz, Larissa, and Ulf Wuggenig. 2005. "Cultural globalization between myth and reality: The case of the contemporary visual arts." *Art-e-Fact: Strategies of Resistance*: w/p.

Candela, Guido, and Antonello E. Scorcu. 1997. "A price index for art market auctions." *Journal of Cultural Economics* 21: pp. 175-196.

Candela, Guido, and Antonello E. Scorcu. 2001. "In search of stylized facts on art market prices: Evidence from the secondary market for prints and drawings in Italy." *Journal of Cultural Economics* 25: pp. 219-231. [doi: 10.1023/A:1010956416307]

Carbonare, Piergiacomo, and Marek Prokůpek. 2020. "Cultural Business Models: The Mistake of Obsoletion." In *Managing the Cultural Business: Avoiding Mistakes, Finding Success,* edited by Michela Addis, and Andrea Rurale. New York: Routledge.

Chanel, Olivier. 1995. "Is art market behaviour predictable?" *European Economic Review* 30, no. 3-4: pp. 519-527. [doi: 10.1016/0014-2921(94)00058-8]

Chong, Derrick. 2009. *Arts management.* New York: Routledge.

Chong, Derrick. 2019. "Art, Finance, Politics, and the Art Museum as a Public Institution." In *Museum Marketization: Cultural Institutions in the Neoliberal Era,* edited by Karin M. Ekström. New York: Routledge.

David, Geraldine, Kim Oosterlinck, and Ariane Szafarz. 2013. "Art market inefficiency." *Economics Letters* 121, no. 1: pp. 23-25. [doi: 10.1016/j.econlet.2013.06.033]

Ekström, Karin M., ed. 2019. *Museum Marketization: Cultural Institutions in the Neoliberal Era.* New York: Routledge.

Eräranta, Kirsi, Johanna Moisander, and Visa Penttilä. 2019. "Reflections on the Marketization of Art in Contemporary Neoliberal Capitalism." In *Museum Marketization: Cultural Institutions in the Neoliberal Era,* edited by Katrin M. Ekström. New York: Routledge.

Frey, Bruno S. 1998. "Superstar museums: An economic analysis." *Journal of cultural economics* 22, no. 2-3: pp. 113-125.

Gamble, Andrew. 2001. "Neo-liberalism." *Capital and Class* 25, no. 3: pp. 127-134. [doi: 10.1177/030981680107500111]

Gérard-Varet, Louis-André. 1995. "On pricing the priceless: Comments on the economics of the visual art market." *European Economic Review* 39, no. 3-4: pp. 509-518. [doi: 10.1016/0014-2921(94)00057-7]

Goetzmann, William N. 1993. "Accounting for taste: Art and the financial markets over three centuries." *The American Economic Review* 83, no. 5: pp. 1370-1376.

Goodwin, James. 2008. *The International Art Markets: the essential guide for collectors and investors.* London: Kogan Page.

Higgs, Helen, and Andrew Worthington. 2005. "Financial returns and price determinants in the Australian art market." *Economic record* 81, no. 253: pp. 113-123. [doi: 10.1111/j.1475-4932.2005.00237.x]

Horowitz, Noah. 2014. *Art of the deal: Contemporary art in a global financial market.* Princeton: Princeton University Press.

Joy, Annamma, and John F. Sherry Jr. 2003. "Disentangling the paradoxical alliances between art market and art world." *Consumption, Markets and Culture* 6, no. 3: pp. 155-181. [doi: 0.1080/1025386032000153759]

Kraeussl, Roman, and R. Logher. 2010. "Emerging art markets." *Emerging Markets Review* 11, no. 4: pp. 301-318. [doi: 10.1016/j.ememar.2010.07.002]

Lee, Kangsan. 2018. "Neoliberal Marketization of Global Contemporary Visual Art Worlds: Changes in Valuations and the Scope of Local and Global Markets." In *Art and the Challenge of Markets Volume 2,* edited by Victoria D. Alexander et al. Cham: Palgrave Macmillan.

McAndrew, Claire. 2020. *The Art Market 2020.* Basel: Art Basel and UBS.

McGuigan, Jim. 2005. "Neo-Liberalism, Culture and Policy." *International Journal of Cultural Policy* 11, no.1: pp. 229-241. [doi: 10.1080/10286630500411168]

Mei, Jianping, and Michael Moses. 2005. "Beautiful Asset: Art as Investment." *Journal of Investment Consulting* 7, no. 2: pp. 45-51.

Moreau, Nathalie, Dominique Sagot-Duvauroux, and Marion Vidal. 2015. *Contemporary art collectors: The unsung influences on the art scenes.* Paris: Open Edition Books.

Myerscough, John. 1988. *The economic importance of the arts in Britain.* London: Policy Studies Institute.

Pesando, James. E. 1993. "Art as an investment: The market for modern prints." *The American Economic Review* 83, no. 5: pp. 1075-1089.

Plaza, Beatriz. 2006. "The return on investment of the Guggenheim Museum Bilbao." *International journal of urban and regional research* 30, no. 2: pp. 452-467. [doi: 10.1111/j.1468-2427.2006.00672.x]

Quemin, Alain. 2006. "Globalization and Mixing in the Visual Arts: An Empirical Survey of 'High Culture' and Globalization." *International Sociology* 21, no. 4: pp. 522–550. [doi: 10.1177%2F0268580906065299]

Reid, Magnus. 2004. *How to buy and sell art.* Crows Nest: Allen & Unwin.

Renneboog, Luc, and Christophe Spaenjers. 2013. "Buying beauty: On prices and returns in the art market." *Management Science* 59, no. 1: pp. 36-53. [doi: 10.2139/ssrn.1352363]

Resch, Magnus. 2015. *Management of art galleries.* London: Phaidon Press Limited.

Rifkin, Jeremy. 2000. *The Age of Access: How the Shift from Ownership to Access is Transforming Capitalism.* London: Penguin.

Robertson, Iain. 2005. *Understanding International Art Markets and Management.* Abingdon: Routledge.

Taylor, Jeffrey. 2017. *Visual Arts Management.* Abingdon: Routledge.

Velthuis, Olav, and Stefano Baia Curioni. 2016. *Cosmopolitan Canvases. Globalization of the Market for Contemporary Art.* Oxford: Oxford University Press.

Zorloni, Alessia. 2013. *The economics of contemporary art.* Berlin: Springer.

Chapter 3

Microeconomic Failures in the Art Market[1]

Irini Liakopoulou

Oklahoma State University/Union College-NY, USA

Abstract

The present work deals with the economic aspects of the art market. Particularly, it explains why the art market does not respect the conditions of perfect competition. The failure in this case is evident when one or more parameters are not met and, therefore, the price in the market differs from marginal cost. From a first analysis, it emerges that the majority of art works are unique, not standardized goods; many times exist barriers to entry or exit to these markets; the fixed costs are very high; the number of operators in the market is rather limited; the consumers do not have perfect information, etc. In all these cases, the price charged in the market differs from that of marginal cost. Diagrams, mathematical and theoretical analysis are the main tools to explain this topic.

Keywords: Art market; barriers to entry; fixed costs; marginal cost; microeconomic failures; perfect competition.

* * *

1. Introduction

Painters, actors, writers, etc., produce artistic goods and services that are purchased and consumed by consumers. To describe the production path of cultural goods, I need to consider some aspects such as the artistic recognition of cultural goods and/or the monetary value of them.

The economics of the artistic goods, therefore, contain and examine: a) The economic value (price, quality, quantity, demand, offer, etc.) and; b) the artistic

[1] The present work is updated as of March 10, 2020.

value (it may not be linked to its economic value, for example, the artistic value of a painting).

The economics of the artistic goods were formed as a specific chapter of the political economy both because economists have approached the themes of art and because critics and artists have approached the themes of economics. The economics of the artistic goods have only recently passed from an object of interest to an object of research, with themes detached from the personal interests of scholars and has become an applied sector of political economy with a high degree of autonomy.

In fact, from the most ancient civilizations until the eighteenth century, culture, shows and art were almost the exclusive product of the courts and aristocratic palaces. Only recently (at the beginning of the twentieth century) did the economy of cultural heritage gain a place in economic analysis. He was J. M. Keynes to offer one of the first organic contributions to the economic analysis of culture. Specifically, he attributed the autonomy of the economy of cultural heritage to the particularity that requires the financing of culture and, therefore, the need for an ad hoc economic analysis. He argues that the state must select those activities deemed worthy of public financial support, with the sole criterion of a "serious purpose and a reasonable prospect of success", and with the absence of controls on the content of cultural production. According to him, indirect instruments represent the most suitable public financial support, that is, the encouragement of cultural consumption carried out, for example, through radio broadcasts, or to the infrastructural intervention and capital supply, essentially the construction and allocation of buildings in which cultural events can be made available to the public, and thanks to which cultural institutions can become financially autonomous (Hauser 1953; Keynes 1936; 1945).

The fundamental themes, which the economics of the artistic goods deals with, are: 1. The relationship between monetary and artistic value; 2.the efficiency of the cultural heritage market; 3.the relationship between the merchant organization and creativity.

The artist, the critic and the market operate in the market for artistic goods. The market uses the price to transmit consumer preferences and choices (for example, consumers of artistic goods ask for one good rather than another on the market, raising the price of the former and decreasing the price of the latter, thus transmitting tastes and preferences to the producer).

The critic and gatekeeper open the door to success for artists through two channels: Absolute and relative criticism. Absolute criticism provides information on the quality level of an artist, etc., while relative criticism deals with information about consumer preferences regarding the characteristics of artistic products.

If it is undeniable that the market tends to influence the artist, it is, however, true that it is compatible with a considerable pluralism, so that experimental, innovative and artistic expressions oriented towards mass consumption can coexist. The cultural market plays, in reality, its role, taking into consideration not only the pessimistic and optimistic approaches but all the nuances that understand and complete this market whether they are negative (I am talking here of any type of restrictions, impediments to free trade, transfer and creation of them, the birth of market failures) or positive (the cultural raising of citizens, the help of young talents to produce cultural works, the support of incomes, etc.).

This means that the art market does not fall within the general context of one of the classic categories that examines political economy and, in particular, its microeconomic trend. As I will demonstrate later, it falls neither in the category of the perfectly competitive market nor in the monopolistic, oligopolistic one. But it presents a category itself by simultaneously gathering characteristics of more than one market, thus forming its autonomy and dynamism in the already complex world of economics.

In the present work, I will concentrate, therefore, on explaining the causes that the art market does not fit with the classic microeconomic forms of the market. Next, I will examine the microeconomic failures that the art market presents, giving greater weight to positive and negative artistic externalities and to the analysis of the meritorious goods.

2. Microeconomic Market Failures. The Case of Artistic Goods

By microeconomic market failures, I mean those situations in which the market, under free competition, does not achieve the optimal allocation of resources and full efficiency (Pareto efficiency or optimality).[2] According to the classical theory of laissez-faire and the neoclassical theory of equilibrium by Walras and Pareto, the market equilibrium in perfect competition achieves an efficient allocation of resources.

---

[2] The Pareto efficiency is a market equilibrium with the best allocation of resources. It is the preferable situation to all the others, where no economic entity is willing to change their choices because they consider them the best possible for themselves.

However, in some cases the markets do not reach the optimal allocation. These situations are called market failures. The main causes of market failures are the following:

a) Growing production returns. If the marginal costs are descriptive, the companies have no interest in equating the price with the marginal cost (p = CMa). Therefore, the market equilibrium diverges from the competitive equilibrium and moves towards monopoly.

b) Externalities. If the actions of an economic entity affect the well-being of the community in a negative (diseconomy) or positive (external economies) way, without being able to identify the manager or the beneficiary, market prices diverge from those of competitive equilibrium.

c) Monopoly. The presence of monopolies distorts the use of resources in a sector, market or economy. The quantity produced is reduced, and the selling price of products and services increases.

d) Public goods. Although some goods and services (called public goods) are useful for the community, they are not produced by private companies on the market because they do not have all the characteristics of economic goods (e.g., health, school, security, defense, etc.). In particular, public goods have the characteristics of non-rivalry[3] and non-exclusion.[4]

e) Imperfect information. Economic operators (households, businesses) do not have access to all the information of the market (prices, quantities, quality, etc.). Information asymmetry situations occur that deviate the market price from the competitive equilibrium.

f) Uncertainty. There are situations of lack of certainty in the market that determine expectations and risk.

g) Bounded rationality. Economic subjects do not always make more rational decisions to maximize their utility and well-being. Therefore, they do not decide in conditions of perfect rationality.

Some of the above failures are present in the art markets. Particularly, in the art market there are public goods; some art markets are absent or incomplete—there are marked inequity and differences in the income of the artists, externalities, meritorious goods, and information asymmetry. In other words,

---

[3] By non-rivalry I mean that the use of public good by one person does not reduce its use by another person (e.g. public order, defense, etc.).

[4] In the non-exclusion case, no individual can be excluded from the enjoyment of the public good, regardless of the price he declares he wants to pay.

these are conditions that do not allow the art market to achieve efficient allocation in production and/or in exchange.

In the following paragraphs, I will analyze such failures that come from the absence of perfect competition, giving particular attention to externalities and meritorious goods. I will pay more attention to these two cases, as they are failures that better characterize and describe the cultural and/or artistic market. Finally, the cases of inequity and information asymmetry will be analyzed as further analytical hypotheses within the contexts of externalities and meritorious goods.

3. Absence of Perfect Competition

A market is called perfectly competitive if it can satisfy (simultaneously) the following characteristics: The product produced must be homogeneous; they must not be barriers to entry and exit in the market; it must be a very large number of operators practicing in the market; there must be no collusion or understanding between the operators that are part of the market and; the information must be symmetric. If these conditions are met, producers and consumers maximize their profits by charging a price equal to the marginal cost (i.e., the increase in the total cost incurred by the producer to create an additional unit of product).

The failure in this case occurs when one or more parameters are not satisfied and, therefore, the market price is different from the marginal cost. Let's see what happens in the case of artistic goods. From a first analysis, it emerges that the majority of the artistic goods do not meet one or more of the above-listed criteria; that is, the majority of the works of art are unique, the artistic goods are not standardized, and many times there are barriers to the entry or exit of these markets. Particularly, the costs of the fixed production factors to create monuments, etc., are very high, so not everyone can produce works of art, become musicians, world-famous artists, etc. This means that the number of operators in the market is rather limited, and the consumers do not have complete and correct information regarding the characteristics and quality of the works of art, musical pieces, etc. Finally, there is the possibility that the artist should collaborate with the critic in order to increase the price of his work in the art market. In all these cases, the price charged on the market is different from that of the marginal cost, and this means that the art market is not perfectly competitive (See: Acocella 2006; Di Maio 1999, 117-120).

4. Failures in the Artistic Job Market

One of the causes of microeconomic market failure that occurs even in the presence of a Pareto optimal is the unequal distribution of income. A Pareto optimal situation can also occur when the final allocations of goods do not allow the survival of some citizens of a country. On the other hand, several economists argue that improving equity can actually increase the efficiency of individuals. Let's see what happens in the artistic job market, that is, if it is represented by inequalities in the distribution of artistic income or not.

To highlight the income distribution system in the art market, it would be better to first define the concept of the term "artist" from an economic point of view. A subject defines himself as an artist when he receives artistic recognition from the company; that is, when the company requests his works and/or his own performances. However, many times the artistic and monetary recognition do not coincide over time; that is, the life cycle of the work can be different from the life cycle of the artist.[5] This diversity creates inequalities in artists' income. The artists, when working as dependents—as are for example the dancers of stable companies or the musicians of stable orchestras—, receive high guarantees of continuity in employment and income of low variability; instead, artists such as painters, sculptors, etc. who are independent, take the risk of a self-employed business by betting on the company's monetary recognition.

In general, the average income of artists that can be obtained—for example, from the sale of works or from public or private grants—is insufficient and, therefore, must be integrated with works in the non-artistic sector. Furthermore, the total remuneration of the artists is on average lower than that of technical-professional workers similar in terms of personal characteristics and professional training time (Hamilton 2000). The main reasons for the low remuneration are the reduced hourly remuneration and the limited working time. Another factor closely related to low remuneration is the high variability of the profits that artists perceive. Both factors push the artists to look for a second job, which guarantees them a stable income over time.

The failures of the artistic job market are justified, for example, with the experience that the artist accumulates over time. The experience, in this case, constitutes an investment and, consequently, the artists with more experience earn higher incomes; or with working age in relation to experience; with the school education of the artist; but above all with the innate talent of the artist which is strengthened by the concentration of the artists' demand on it as well as by the help of technology (for example, high-quality audio reproductions help increase sales). The latter is perhaps the most suitable explanation for explaining the failures regarding the artists' income, but it does not exclude the

---

[5] The link between artistic value and income is present not only for durable works but also for visual works of art. (Abbing 2002; Behhamou 2001)

partial validity of the other explanations, which are not alternatives to it (Adler 1985; Behhamou 2001, 38-39; Caves 2001, 99ss; Frey 2000; Rosen 1981).

5. Transaction Costs and Information Imperfections: Asymmetric, Incomplete and Information Impossibility

In the economics of art, transaction costs prevail; that is, the costs inherent in the organization and functioning of the art markets. In these markets, the transaction costs derive from the difficulties of monitoring the production process and evaluating the artistic and/or cultural output. They are especially accentuated in the case of the stipulation of contracts between the producer of cultural and artistic services and the consumer, in cases where there is a high degree of uncertainty about the future output, which makes future consumption and the act of exchange itself uninsurable. These services are rarely consumed occasionally, while most of the time they are exchanged. Moreover, the most relevant characteristic of them is the continuity of the service provided. The continuous transaction requires the non-specification of the contents of the services, which are the object of the transaction. Therefore, this type of contract contains a strong IT content which is not fully revealed by consumers, which means entering into the contract implies not only higher transaction costs but also a high content of asymmetric information (Hodgson 1988; Krashinsky 1986).

By information asymmetry, I mean the different information available for the two parties (for example, the creator of a work of art and the eventual buyer) between which there could be an exchange. In this case, the creator of a work of art is the agent, that is, the individual who has complete information and any buyer assumes the role of the principal, that is, the individual who does not have complete information. According to the information problem, one of the two parties, the one that does not have perfect information, relies on the other to carry out transactions that have unobservable aspects.

Asymmetric information can create an adverse selection situation, that is, a situation where the principal cannot observe important characteristics, before making the exchange, regarding the quality of the work of art, or on the seriousness and artistic recognition of him, or on situations in which the principal himself may find himself. On the contrary, if the principal is unable to observe important characteristics after the conclusion of the exchange, such as when he is unable to observe the actions performed by the agent or the characteristics of the artistic work supplied by him, we are faced with the case of moral hazard.

The problems of adverse selection and moral hazard are even more evident in the case of joint production (that is, when production normally takes place in a group and is the result of the coordination of several factors) in cultural activities (Trimarchi 1993, 78). For example, the execution of musical pieces by a choir (they assume the role of the agents in this case),[6] in which the same part must be performed by a more or less large group of artists, creates problems regarding the objective contribution of each musician to the final product. The conductor (assumes the main part) can improve the performance of the musical pieces, correcting the errors and imperfections only in part and only after the error has been made (that is, only after one of the choristers has failed to respect all or part of the technical production rules). The role of the conductor (of the supervisor and principal), however, is diminished when the record companies make continuous corrections and several recording sessions or even use acoustic tricks to improve the artistic quality of the musical pieces. In the latter case, however, the element of the contextuality of production and consumption is lacking, and the conductor assumes an important role in determining the quality of the product. This situation favors, in the end, as in any other production case, any unfair behavior (Alchian and Demsetz 1972; Arrow 1985a; Arrow 1985b; McManus 1975).

The art sector not only encounters information problems before or after bargaining (in the case of shows, artistic works, etc.) but also because of the uniqueness of the product (in the case of the visual arts) and in general at all stages of distribution (quality and benchmarks) of the goods and services in question.

In such cases, the presence of a mediator who can offer rather complete information about the quality and artistic content of the artistic goods and services in question is considered favorable. This task is usually carried out by artistic critics since the information provided by them can constitute an important indication for the public of consumers that can improve their quality as well as the evaluation of consumers for the goods and services in question (reduction of evaluation risk).

Besides the information asymmetry and incompleteness, the so-called information impossibility is highlighted in the artistic sector. In this case, cultural and artistic institutions know the particularities of the materials, personnel, means of production, etc. who use and cannot do anything to improve any errors, defects, etc., while consumers derive utility from their ignorance on the potential transformation of the game, even if they are aware

[6] In this case, the presence of a chief agent is not necessarily verified, since it is a work that is carried out in a group and, by carrying out joint work, each of them has relevant information on the characteristics or conduct of the other members, or also on the characteristics of the physical resources used in that production, compared to what external parties may know about them. (Liakopoulou 2009)

that the possible results will not always result positive for them, being able to prove useless without this being evident from any element prior to actual consumption.

The impossibility of information therefore requires a completely peculiar strategic reaction, which generally consists in abandoning divergent behaviors, and in taking on, alongside signals aimed at demonstrating the reputational level of the operators, of cooperative choices, due to the common knowledge of the subjects regarding the limitation of the same information impossibility (Hansmann 1981; Trimarchi 1990).

6. Artistic Goods

By public goods, I mean those goods for which the conditions of exclusion (for the consumer or for the producer) from the use of a good and rivalry do not apply, that is, the reduction of availability of a good used by a consumer or producer to others operators. Let's see if these conditions are manifested in the art market. In the case of musical, theatrical performances, exhibitions, etc., the condition of non-exclusion does not apply, as to see the show, the exhibition, etc., the consumer must pay the entrance ticket. Furthermore, there is a technical exclusion, which is given by the inability to jointly access the visit of the property, show, etc. (therefore you need time and money to visit, follow and access these goods and services) (Dell'Orso 2002; Luciani 1992). This condition is met in the case of shows in the square, but in these cases, the choice of the event depends on public bodies, public administration, etc. The latter make this choice (they assume the costs of use) considering the asset in question not as a public but as a meritorious asset. Merit goods are defined as those goods or services to which the community attributes a particular functional value to the moral and social development of the community itself: Think of reading good books or attending valid musical and theatrical performances etc. Often the public operator satisfies these needs regardless of a specific demand from citizens, but as a consequence of the evaluation of the advantages that the whole society can derive from it. At other times, public action, within this particular category of goods or services, is carried out through the prohibition of having a certain behavior, such as smoking in public places. Some economists (for example, Brosio) define meritorious goods as mixed public goods whose public component benefits more or less restricted segments of the population (for example, subsidies for music or expenses for the conservation of artistic heritage). Much of the literature frequently and widely refers to the concept of merit goods when trying to explain the reasons for public intervention (Brosio 1998, 143). The only case that I can consider as a public good are the shows that are held in festivals—where the source of funding comes from citizens—or, in the case of artistic goods, located in open spaces accessible to all and where exclusion, both economic and technical, seems impossible or highly expensive, such as the Circus Maximus.

However, there are cases of goods that are privately owned but their conservation is the responsibility of the State, such as the buildings in the Piazza di Spagna or cases of goods that are public property but their conservation is up to private individuals as was the Villa Borghese in Italy in the past (Curzi 2004).

7. Artistic Externalities

The more widespread in society is culture, arts, cultural events, theatrical and musical performances, the more they bring benefits to consumers and subsequently to the whole community. These positive effects that derive from the consumption of artistic goods and services are not limited only to those who are willing to pay to enjoy them, but they spread to the benefit of much wider classes of the community, as is the case for the benefits, for example of a well-planned urban landscape. (Robbins 1963) In this case, the community is back from a positive externality that has been created by artistic consumption.[7]

In general terms, the act of externality occurs in the artistic and cultural sector when the activity of artistic and/or cultural production or consumption of a lover of culture and/or art influences, negatively or positively, the well-being of another individual, without the latter receiving compensation (in the case of a negative impact-negative externality) or paying a price (in the case of a positive impact-positive externality) equal to the cost or benefit borne/received.

The externalities manifested in the art market can be of two types: positive and negative. Positive externalities occur when an individual's activities (of cultural and/or artistic production and/or consumption) are associated with positive effects towards other individuals (artists, artistic, entertainment, consumers, etc.), and the latter do not pay a price equal to the benefits received. Examples of positive cultural and/or artistic externalities are, for example, the decision of a theater company to activate acting courses (training of skilled workers), the creation of a monument in the center of a large city which constitutes a tourist attraction, etc. However, in order to be able to affirm with certainty that what has been described represents an external aspect, I should affirm with equal certainty that, for example, the number of visitors to that cultural monument is completely independent of the quality and quantity of accommodation. The negative cultural and/or artistic externality is manifested, however, when an individual's activity (of production and/or

[7] Externalities produce both public and private goods.

consumption) is associated with negative effects towards other individuals (consumers, businesses, etc.) and the individual responsible for the effects does not correspond to the injured party a price equal to the cost suffered. Examples of artistic externalities are the noise pollution of musical events, of pop, rock, classical, etc. concerts, or the pollution caused by some materials used in the production of an artistic work.

In the case of positive externalities, the activity of the artist, of the artistic and/or cultural enterprises, of the consumers of the art with which the external diseconomy is associated will be pushed to a level higher than the socially efficient level. In the case of positive externalities, however, the artistic and/or cultural production/consumption activity to which the external economy is associated will be pushed to a level lower than the socially efficient level, i.e., lower than the level to which the individual would have it if it had been remunerated by the beneficiaries.

I can present the concept of cultural and/or artistic externalities in formal terms. In fact, externalities are the cause of divergence between private and social costs, that is, between the private marginal product and the social marginal product. In the presence of external economies, the private marginal cost is greater than the social one, i.e., the social marginal benefits (SMgB) are equal to the sum of the private marginal benefits (PMgB) plus the external marginal benefits. External diseconomies mean, on the other hand, that the private marginal cost is lower than the social one; that is, in the case of negative externalities, the social marginal cost (SMgC) is equal to the sum of the private marginal cost (PMgC) plus the external marginal damages (see Figure 3.1).

Figure 3.1 | Representation of Marginal Costs and Benefits

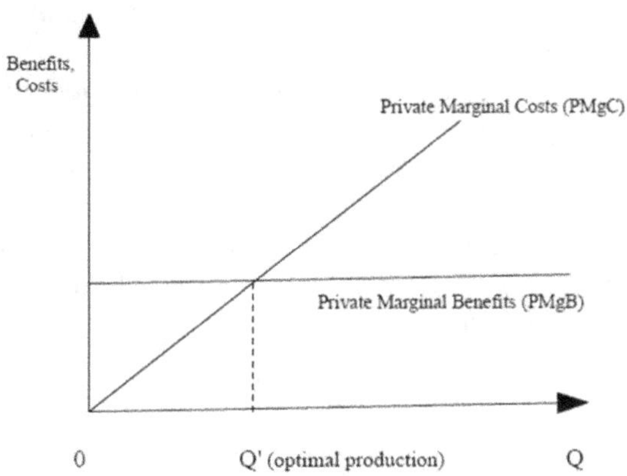

Representation made by the author.

I consider now an artistic enterprise operating in a competitive market, where PMgB = Constant Marginal Revenues = Price received for each unit produced/sold. Furthermore, the production costs incurred by the company are presented by the total private costs (TPC (Q)) function. Suppose that marginal private costs are rising (PMgC). I can see in the graph the artistic enterprise that chooses the optimal production level Q (the one that allows you to maximize the profits of the artistic enterprise) comparing benefits and costs. What I want to see at this point is whether this optimal production level achieved is also socially optimal. That is, if a shift in the optimal production level would provide society with greater benefits than costs.

Figure 3.2 | Total Damages

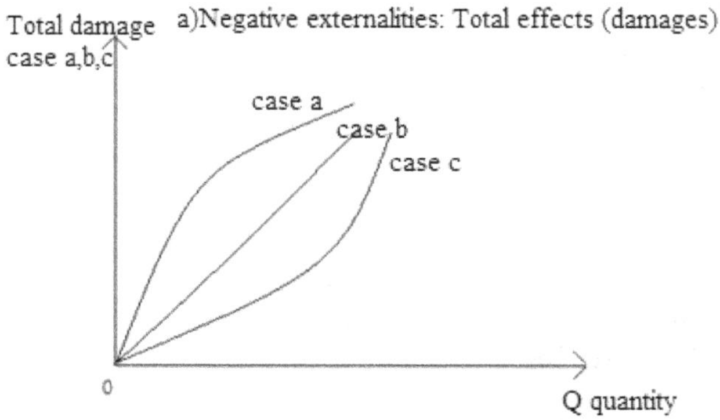

Representation made by the author.

To answer this question, I consider that: a) The artistic enterprise causes noise pollution (case A); b) that the damages related to noise pollution (external diseconomies D (Q)), expressed as a function of the production level) are borne by other individuals (people who do not like listening to loud music) (case B); c) that the artistic company does not bear any cost for noise pollution (case C). If the previous conditions are met, we are faced with a case of negative externalities. The production costs incurred, therefore, by the artistic enterprise (total private costs TPC) do not coincide with the social costs (total social costs TSC), that is: TPC (Q) <TSC (Q). I represent the results (total and marginal damages) in the following graphs (see Figures 3.2 and 3.3).

Figure 3.3 | Marginal Damages

b)Negative externalities: (Total) marginal effects

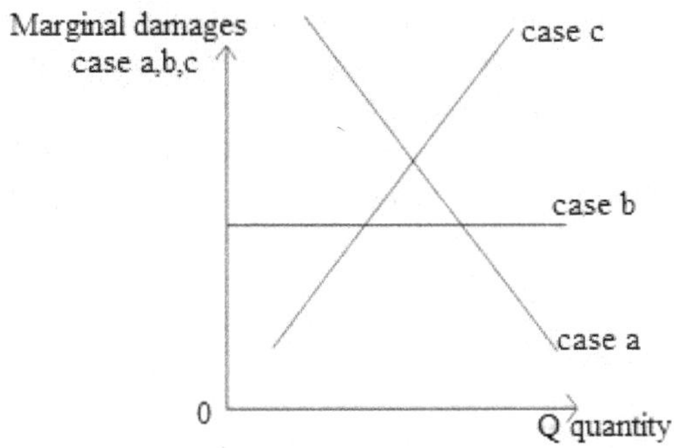

Representation made by the author.

Consider the third case where marginal damage is increasing to identify the socially optimal production level Q * (see Figure 3.4). The social marginal cost curve (SMgC) is nothing more than the sum of the external marginal damage curve (EMgD) and the private marginal cost curve (PMgC), that is: SMgC = EMgD + PMgC.

Figure 3.4 | Socially Optimal Production

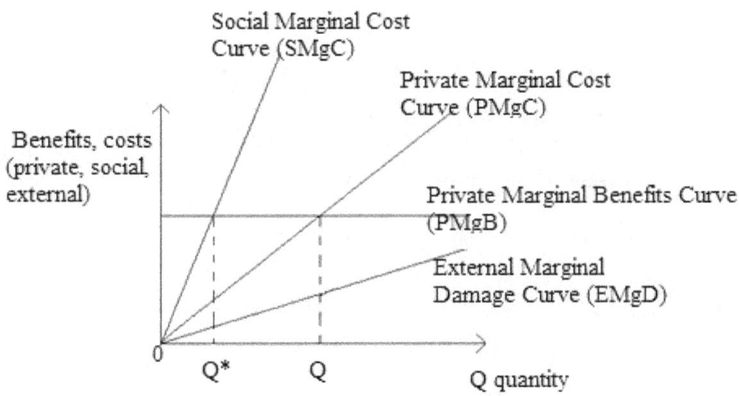

Representation made by the author.

I will see through an example why the passage from Q to Q * (Q => Q *) implies an improvement in allocative efficiency. By allocative efficiency, in Pareto terms, I mean that possibility, in fact, of getting more than something (in our case, in terms of decreasing noise pollution to satisfy one or more individuals) without having to have less- or even having even more than anything else (satisfaction of the artistic endeavor), with given availability. While I speak of excellence in an allocative sense if, however, I move from it, it is not possible to improve the satisfaction of someone (of the pollutants in our case) without worsening the satisfaction of at least one other member of the community (of the artistic enterprise) (Acocella 2006; Gravelle and Rees 1981; Pareto 1906). I will demonstrate, therefore, why it would be socially convenient to move from a quantity point offered in the market Q to a lower one Q * (I will use a general example, not the application of a certain policy such as taxation, negotiable rights, etc.).

Let's assume that:

- the total private benefits (TPB (Q)) are: TPB (Q) = 400Q;
- the private marginal benefits (PMgB (Q)) are: PMgB (Q) = 400;
- total private costs (TPC (Q)) are: TPC (Q) = 20Q2;
- the private marginal costs (PMgC (Q)) are: 40Q;
- the external costs (total damages) (EstC. (Q)) are: EstC. (Q) = 4,5Q2;
- the increasing marginal external costs (increasing marginal damages) (Est.MgC (Q)) are: Est.MgC (Q) = 10Q

I also assume that the production level chosen by the theater company is Q = 10. Let's now calculate the net benefits of the theater company and the amount of loss (noise pollution) of the subjects:

PMgB (Q) = PMgC (Q) => 400 = 40Q => Q = 10 (1); PTB (Q) = 400 * Q = 400 * 10 = 4000 (2) STC = TPC (Q) + Est.C
(Q) = 20Q2 + 4.5Q2 = 20 * 102 + 4.5 * 102 = 2000 + 450 = 2450 (3)
(2)- (3) => TPB (Q) -TSC = 4000-2450 = 1550 (net balance) (4)

The net benefits of the theater company are:

TPB (Q) - TPC (Q) = 400Q-20Q2 = 400 * 10-20 * 102 = 4000-2000 = 2000 (5)

Loss of pollutants:

(net balance minus the net benefits of the theater company) 1550-2000 = -450 (6)

Let's now calculate the net benefits of the theater company and the losses of the polluting subjects according to a socially optimal production level Q * to internalize noise pollution) (Q = 8, see point (7)). To obtain the socially optimal level of production I use the following formula:

PMgB(Q*)=PMgC(Q*)+Est.MgC(Q*) => 400=40Q*+10Q* => 400=50Q* => Q*=8 (7)
TPB(Q*)=400Q*=400*8=3200 (8)
TSC=TPC(Q*)+Est.C
(Q*)=20Q*2+4,5Q*2=20*82+4,5*82=1280+288=1568 (9)
(8)-(9) => 3200-1568=1632 (net balance) (10)

the net benefits for the theater company are:

TPB(Q*)-TPC(Q*)=400Q*-20Q*2=400*8-20*82=3200-1280=1920(11)
pollutant losses: 1632- 1920=-288 (12)

Therefore, passing from Q to Q * the theater company that causes noise pollution would lose 80, (11) - (5) = 1920-2000 = -80 while the pollutants will have a gain equal to: (-288- (-450)) = 162. The net profit will be equal to: 162-80 = 82, i.e. the passage from Q to Q + would imply an improvement in the allocation of resources equal to 82.

There are, therefore, two elements that characterize externalities: a) The interdependence of individual cultural actions and; b) the absence of a cultural and/or artistic market since there is no voluntary exchange as well as regulatory prices to define the cultural exchange (Lambertini and Orsini 1988; Randon 2002; Tirelli 2005; Tullock 1997). In these cases, the need to correct external effects is considered indispensable. Corrective public intervention is essential and derives from considerations of economic efficiency.

Particularly, in artistic goods and services, the act of externality derives, first of all, from the prestige a country enjoys from the conservation of its cultural heritage. In this case, the presence of the State is considered indispensable: in the case of positive externalities to broaden the positive cultural effects caused in society, while in the case of negative externalities to internalize/reduce the negative effects. This can be done in various ways, namely through: regulation; subsidization (taxation) of cultural and/or artistic activities from which external economies (diseconomies) arise; the incentive to eliminate external diseconomies and the introduction of negotiable rights to the creation of external diseconomies.

a) regulation: These are direct control measures with which certain obligations or prohibitions are normally imposed on artists (producers) and consumers (regarding permissive and/or prohibitive rules at international, community and internal level, see the paragraph on the limitations of import, export, circulation of cultural and/or artistic goods and services) (Attali 1978; Eisenberg 1997). In music festivals, simple taxation—in the presence of sufficiently rigid demand—would have the effect of transferring a large part of the burden directly to consumers, and for this reason, it does not seem practicable. A possible way out would be to allocate a portion of the proceeds from copyright and rights related to the financing of concert activities. The asymmetrical distribution of the income procured by rights seems to suggest that there are possibilities of withdrawal without prejudice to the incentives generated by the same rights on the population of authors and publishers. Another solution is VAT, i.e., the rate paid on phonographic products. The artists request the lowering of the rate, also due to the inequitable treatment compared to other cultural products. This situation causes some commercial distortions since the majority of phonographic products are sold on newsstands. The idea of allocating a fixed amount of this tax to the financing of musical performances could justify the need for the greater tax burden and, at the same time, to rebalance the conflicting relationship between representation and repetition.

It is the most common tool for controlling externalities. In order to be efficient (to comply with the standards proposed by the various laws, regulations, etc.), this tool also requires the presence of a controller who has the power to impose fines in the event of infringements.

The results of regulation may be similar to those derived from other "internalization" measures on a static level, in that it tends to internalize external diseconomies and increase efficiency. The results may, however, be dissimilar when the available information is incomplete and/or incorrect. It seems to be a rather preferable measure than the others as it requires lower administrative costs if uniform regulation is used.

b) the case of subsidization/taxation of cultural and/or artistic activities: A subsidy is proposed for artistic and/or cultural businesses that introduce tools to reduce noise pollution, for example. The aim of the subsidy is to encourage change towards low noise pollution technologies.[8] In the case of positive externalities, the State with its presence can, therefore, through the use of subsidies to further increase the benefits of its citizens, for example, in a situation of not full employment of the factors for the production of artistic

[8] Usually, in the short term, the subsidy reduces the noise pollution of the band. In the long run, however, there may be an increase in noise pollution deriving from the sector because, subsidies increase the net benefits of businesses and, therefore, can attract new singers, musical groups, musicians, etc. in the sector that expands the offer and therefore the pollution. (Antonelli 1978; Cowen 1988; Lin 1976)

goods and services by granting subsidies regarding the influx of external demand which increases real income without affecting the price level. In terms of the balance of payments, subsidies regarding the conservation of a country's cultural heritage can stimulate the influx of foreign tourists and, with them, the increase in foreign currencies. Any political cost adopted for the use of these goods is offset, for example, by withdrawals on the activities that benefit from the greatest foreign demand. The positive influence is transmitted not only in the citizens of a country but also in future generations of it,[9] especially in cases of priceless monuments not only for present but also for future generations.

In the case of taxation, it is sufficient to introduce a tax equal to the value of externalities to internalize it. In the case of fixed quantity taxes, tax (I) should be added to the private marginal cost. In this case, the musical group would decide to play the music for which MPC + I = p, where p represents the price of the service (playing the music or/and singing in the audience) in question. Let us now suppose a musical group operating in the perfectly competitive market that generates negative externalities in I * Q for each additional unit produced. Reinterpreting figure 3.4, we see the effects before and after the public intervention. In the place of the external marginal damage curve, I now assign the value I * Q; in the place of the private marginal benefit curve, I assign the price P. The private marginal cost (PMC) curve remains the same, and the social marginal cost curve now represents the PMC + I * Q. Without public intervention, the musical group would play up to the OQ point. If the externality were internalized, by charging the I * Q tax for each additional unit produced, the private marginal cost would be equal to the social cost and the quantity produced would be reduced to OQ * (see Figure 3.4).

c) the incentive: In this case, the State grants a subsidy for the lack of production, that is, the value of the diseconomy in the point of optimal social, for each unit produced less by the company. The short-term result is the same that would have been obtained through a tax commensurate with the quantity produced. In the long run, however, the level of external diseconomy produced by industry may be higher, due to the entry of new musical groups and the increase in the musical performance produced (Baumol and Oates 1975; Stiglitz 1988, 249).

d) introduction of negotiable permits: In this case, in order to efficiently allocate its resources, the music market requires the establishment, for example, of a fixed number of negotiable noise pollution permits. Suppose that

---

9 "We develop programs for the conservation of natural resources and for the improvement of architecture, in part because few of us want to take responsibility for passing on to future generations a country whose beauty has been destroyed" (Baumol and Bowen 1966).

the State is able to accurately assess the level of noise pollution caused by music festivals, music concerts, musicians who play loud in open places, etc. In this case, to achieve the objective of environmental quality, the government can issue a number of negotiable noise pollution permits equal to the maximum desired level of pollution and distribute them to musicians, bands, etc., in question. Starting from this initial allocation, the competitive exchange of permits determines their efficient allocation among industrial companies. To demonstrate effectiveness, I use the Edgeworth box.

Consider the music market consisting of two pop music groups and an Edgeworth box in which I represent the work of the singers on the ascent axis and the number of permits negotiable on that of the ordinates. The height of the Edgeworth box represents the total number of negotiable permits allocated by the government. Each point of the Edgeworth box shows a certain job allocation and negotiable permissions between the two pop music groups (see Figure 3.5).

Figure 3.5 | Edgeworth Box

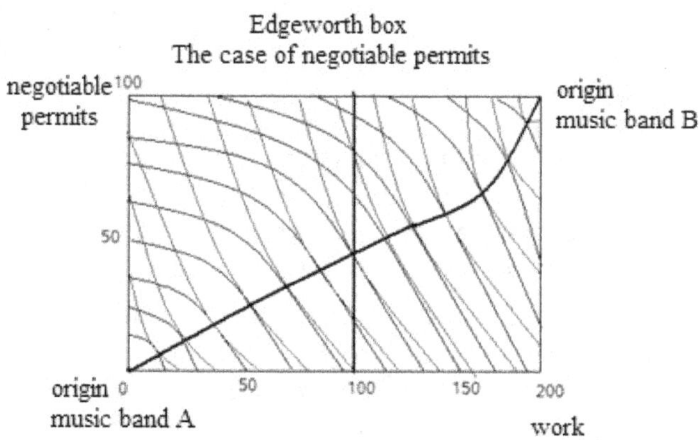

The Edgeworth box represents the allocative efficiency of consumption.
(Acocella 2006, 49)

I also consider that the two musical groups have the same initial work budget. In this case, the initial allocation coincides with the vertical line positioned in the center of the diagram. I see that the competitive exchange of negotiable permits between the two musical groups leads to an allocation belonging to the contract curve,[10] regardless of the position of the initial allocation. Obviously, the initial allocation of permits influences the distribution of the surplus, but the competitive exchange is able to eliminate any efficiency from the market.

I have also seen from the analysis carried out so far that the interdependence of individual cultural preferences and the formation of tastes and dynamic preferences over time constitute the variants that justify the presence of positive or negative externalities in the art market. But when artistic consumption is attributed with characteristics such as that of a mediator to increase and spread the heritage of knowledge and culture and participate in technological and/or paternalistic progress and innovation that cancels or reduces behavior deemed asocial, then such consumption no longer falls within the canons of externalities but most likely in the analysis of the meritorious goods.

8. Artistic Merit Goods

The presence of meritorious goods in the art market emerges when consumers of culture and art do not have information on substantial aspects for their choices and, they have incomplete and incorrect (distorted) information from advertising or other external influences and when the latter do not use the canons of rationality (for example, they are passive, weak and unwilling to make decisions about their future, or those who underestimate their future) to make their own choices (Musgrave 1959; Musgrave 1987; Tittmuss 1963).

When these conditions occur, the State assumes an active (paternalistic) role both in the production and supply of artistic goods and in their consumption. But also private individuals and those who consume artistic goods in general contribute to promoting the arts and their knowledge and finance, albeit partially, the conservation and protection of these goods. However, the presence of the meritorious goods leads, in the majority of cases, to public subsidies, and tax exemptions, incentives, subsidies and concessions of any kind in favor of carrying out these activities.

Public presence is therefore justified by the correction of imperfect rationality and by guaranteeing citizens the consumption of goods of high artistic quality. This presence can correct defects of imperfect rationality through the imposition of restrictions that do not reduce citizens' freedom of choice, which

---

[10] The allocative efficiency of consumption is represented in the Edgeworth box as a set of points of tangency of the indifference curves of the two musical groups in question. This representation highlights the allocations of goods between the two musical groups, distinguishing the optimal ones from those that are not.

means that the State must offer meritorious goods in conditions of competition between multiple private and public producers.

Imperfect rationality is justified in different ways, for example, as a lack of will from the citizens to make current choices due to distorted information or when citizens have difficulty making choices that involve future generations. Citizens do not know if the choices made in the present are able to satisfy future subjects in the best way. The hypothesis that the present subject considers the future in the same way in which they consider future subjects is not easy to demonstrate. This difficulty often pushes the citizens of a country to improve their living conditions in the present and in the future, bringing their lives closer but not that far in time. Such behavior cannot be rational and, moreover, fair since it entails a disadvantage towards future generations (Parfit 1989; Sen 1986). For example, I cannot consider the decision of the citizens of a country fair, who renounce the social security system of future generations or when they accept rules that imply excessive burdens for the future generation. To face these difficulties, it is necessary to constrain (with the appropriate legislation) the choices of the present citizens (Brennan and Buchanan 1990).

This difficulty is also explained by the insufficient information regarding future (cultural and artistic needs in our case) needs. Many times the lack of information pushes citizens to turn to institutions, specialized subjects in order to obtain the necessary information or ask the State directly for the use of the good or service in question. In the latter case, the state covers its expenses through taxation that affects citizens who use these goods or services.

Insufficient information also exists when individuals find it difficult to acquire the information necessary to satisfy their needs. The high or prohibitive purchase cost makes the presence of the state indispensable. The high cost of a restoration technique indispensable for the conservation of a monument requires the intervention and work of public institutions.

Finally, the insufficiency of information is linked to a philosophical, ethical question; that is, the more information acquired, the more availability the individual has to achieve his or her choices. It is interesting, at this point, to highlight Socrates' syllogism regarding the question under consideration.

He prefers philosophy to the game of morra, because he has a greater ability to prove usefulness than the proletarian and that gives greater satisfaction than this to those who have developed their sensitivity and intelligence. He has, on the margin, a higher marginal utility, because he has a greater capacity for enjoyment and, therefore, achieves a greater total utility. His dissatisfaction, therefore, does not prevent him from preferring his own state, because he gives him more globally (Hare 1984, 31).

The task of the State is, in this case, to provide more citizens with the possibility of obtaining more superior cultural assets. Obtaining cultural training broadens the range of preferences of citizens and changes them over time. However, the question becomes rather complicated in that a high level of acculturation hides the true preferences of individuals, which derive from ethical preferences[11] and strictly personal interests. The lack of individual autonomy in the case of choices involving the use of meritorious goods is rather marked. The substitution of individuals by the State regarding the fulfillment of choices that require the use of meritorious goods binds individual autonomy[12] on the one hand and safeguards it on the other (Forte 1993; Hausman and McPherson 1993).

When the preferences of the subjects are not forced and bound by the State, the merit goods that impose themselves to a different extent than that desired by the consumer are (under democratic processes) legitimate. Legitimacy is not synonymous with fulfilling citizens' needs as the resources to produce them are scarce and, therefore, the State must make further choices to determine and refine the ordering of these preferences as well as the budgetary policies to be followed.

9. Conclusions

As I have demonstrated in the previous paragraphs, I cannot identify a case of market failure that occurs in all cases of artistic goods and services. I have already illustrated, albeit briefly, the importance of public presence and some methods of intervention in particular cases of failures (externalities, meritorious goods). This happens, as I have already seen, when the market fails to achieve the optimal allocation of resources, and the State, consequently, is justified to intervene in the economy with action and interventions to correct the malfunction.

---

[11] These are those situations in which individuals accept certain values or preferences such as the protection of historical places, of the environment, etc. even when their preferences may differ. These ethical preferences are the result of a historical process of interaction between the subjects that has led to the formulation of common values or preferences that are transmitted over time (Musgrave 1987, 187).

[12] The replacement of consumer sovereignty by the state, at first sight, seems to make the weight of citizens attributed to the vote as an expression of consensus over time, marginal or null. Analyzing in depth this syllogism we will discover that things are different, that is, in reality, politicians perceive and anticipate certain objectives, with respect to citizens' preferences, seeking the answer on retrospective popular consensus (Chiacone and Osculati 1993).

In particular, public intervention in support of culture mainly concerns the nature of the good, which can be a merit good, a public good or/and a good that has important externalities. When one or more of these phenomena occur in artistic markets, the interventions are considered necessary and are manifested in the following ways: by regulation (regulation is nothing more than a set of laws and norms which have as their objective to protect the art market, i.e., artists and consumers of art, to transmit information aimed at improving the functioning of the art market, as well as a tool to provide adequate incentives to administrators of artistic institutions. The rules, laws, etc. dictations usually have a permissive character when they promote the protection of certain rights and prohibitive when they prevent certain behaviors such as, for example, restrictions on the sale of visual works abroad. In the case of production and consumption, the rules are sometimes introduced to protect the domestic industry; for example, there is an obligation to transmit at least a certain share of national and European productions in the schedules of European televisions or to protect the rights of authors); through grants and transfers in currency or in the form of goods and services (subsidies in production and sometimes also in consumption aim to increase efficiency, that is to resolve a market failure present in consumption or production. However, this tool creates equity problems as it forces citizens who do not want to consume artistic products and services to contribute through the tax levy on art. The subsidies can be paid in different ways, intensity and quality such as fixed sum subsidies, those paid by private institutions, subsidies linked to the sale of access tickets, in the form of vouchers distributed to consumers and those of a nature (in the form of goods and services). These forms of delivery of subsidies cause different effects on sales policies, internal organization and production techniques, etc. For example, fixed-form subsidies are neutral with respect to the economic choices of the subjects but strengthen the public role in the process of selection, while the subsidies in kind, apart from the direct effect they cause on the production process, allow better dissemination of information and help to build the reputation of young artists thus improving the selection process, avoiding clientelisms and, removing requests of that part of show creators who just want to collect public funding); through taxes[13] and tax exemptions granted to those who make bequests or donations;[14] through

---

[13] In such cases, the σtate introduces a fixed tax to internalize the negative effects caused by the action of producers and/or consumers of art.

[14] Different is the case of tax exemptions made by bequests or donations. It is a form of indirect subsidy which is motivated by the objective of offering more opportunities to those who create or, more generally, offer works of art. Usually, the impact of these tax deductions is not easy to capture, however its effectiveness, at least with reference to the

artistic training and education, from the dissemination of news about the cultural market. Public support for education and artistic training is relevant to the dissemination of information regarding the current situation of the art market. For example, responsible for the current situation and future of art education in Italy is the Ministry of Education, University and Research. It proposes new programs, strategies and modifications both in high school and at university in order to develop and raise the quality of the analysis on current school situations, to focus the educational and training purposes and to identify the consequent educational didactic assumptions. In order to achieve these objectives, it very often finds the restlessness of the contracting parties in front of the cut of funds for artistic training and research in the cultural field as well as programming for some without ends and well-defined hierarchies at school and university level and; the protection the rights of authors, publishers and artists in general (a particular type of public intervention constitutes the legal protection of authors). It guarantees authorship and economic exploitation of the work. The first property protects the moral ownership and integrity of the work. It is a universal and alienable right since it guarantees the moral ownership of all artists. The ownership, however, concerns the economic and commercial sphere of works of art reproducible in copies, CDs, DVDs, books, etc. This is a transferable right (from the author to the publisher) that may concern: a) The creation of an annuity on all copies sold; b) the one-off sale of all rights and; c) verification of both possibilities. In this case, they are paid to the author (or his heirs) for 50 years starting from the date of first publication of the work. After the expiry of the right, the work becomes public domain and reproducible without payment of copyright, which retains only the authorship). However, public intervention does not always eliminate or internalize the failures of the art market; in such a case, the presence/action of the private is welcomed.

At a theoretical level, I can note the Coase theorem, where, in the presence of externalities, individuals can overcome the problems of allocative inefficiency thanks to the free negotiation of property rights between them and without public intervention. This solution is independent of the initial distribution of these rights as, for example, it happens in the case of a musical group that produces musical pieces and during the execution of them causes noise pollution to the surrounding community. A musical group in the presence of negative externalities will be willing to give up production if it obtains a payment higher than the difference between benefits and costs. The company, for its part, could offer the musical group a certain sum to abstain from

---

donor, is given by a third of the total public expenditure allocated to art and culture and is financed in this way. (Peacock and Rizzo 1994, 177)

production, as long as this sum is less than the damage caused by noise pollution. The bargaining between the two parties will allow reaching the optimal production level both for the musical group and for the community.

In other cases, the failures of the art market can be reduced or eliminated through the introduction of rules that penalize the behavior of agents operating in that market, or thanks to the intergenerational agreement, i.e., sensitizing and empowering the present generations for future ones.

In still other cases, the public presence could be characterized as harmful when, for example, it follows the interests of lobbies or politicians at the expense of cultural action and artistic creation. Many times this policy hides exclusion, denial, marginalization behaviors from the market of some schools of thought, artistic movements, etc. which are contrary to the political regime or reflect the propaganda of the government, as happened for example with the Stalinist dictatorship which imposed socialist realism in order to educate its people (Frey 2000, 8; Magarotto 1980; Manacorda 1942; Rose-Ackerman 1986).

Finally, in some cases, the failure caused by public intervention is higher than that caused by the market. This situation occurs when the state subsidizes artistic activities that do not run into deficits, in which case the subsidy action reduces the incentive of the cultural activity organizers to increase their income. These distortions must be reduced or eliminated when the subsidy is fixed, in monetary terms or in the provision of artistic services, such as the concession of a museum or an exhibition space (Frey and Pommerehne 1991).

In all the previous inefficiencies, and not only the State seeks, therefore, to contain the intervention/action of private individuals. In formal terms, private intervention is presented under three forms, such as patronage; funding of cultural institutions for advertising purposes; and the financing of cultural institutions by private individuals.

In the first case, private companies but above all families support art without expecting an economic return. In this case, the funding has a meritorious character and is attributed to support a nation, a social group, an institution, an artist, etc. The patron usually to promote and increase the artistic heritage, the culture of a nation, etc. leaves a large space of freedom of movement, action, and artistic creation to the producer. On the other hand, the artist proposes an artistic project that highlights the artistic quality of it, and consequently, the possibility of its actual realization (De Giorgi 1988; Graziani et al. 1992).

In the second case, private companies finance cultural and/or artistic activities that do not directly relate to their production process. In this case, the financing of cultural institutions is indirect in nature and aims to increase the image and prestige of the company where, through a monetary consideration, the company expects to increase its profits. Funding is provided to artists, shows, etc. of world renown, rather than on little known actors or subjects, because the risk assumed is higher and the result on sales of the firm is uncertain (De Sanctis 2006; Bucci et al. 2003; Frignani et al. 1993; Onofri 2003; Tellarini 1997).

Finally, in the third and last case, private companies finance cultural institutions, as they are directly part of the production process. The cultural product can be produced both outside and within the company. In any case, the cultural product constitutes the input to the production process and to the profit of the company. An example of this case is the lighting company iGuzzini, which specialized in setting up (Bondardo Comunicazione 2000; Lux 1973).

References

Abbing, Hans. 2002. *Why Are Artist Poor?*. Amsterdam: Amsterdam University Press.

Acocella, Nicola. 2006. *Fondamenti di politica economica.* Roma: Carocci.

Adler, Moshe. 1985. "Stardom and Talent." *American Economic Review* 75, no. 1: pp. 208-212.

Alchian, Armen and Harold Demsetz. 1972. "Production, Information Costs, and Economic Organization." *American Economic Review* 62, no. 5: pp. 777-795.

Antonelli, Cristiano. 1978. *Economie esterne e sentiero di crescita dell'impresa.* Torino: Giappichell.

Arrow, Kenneth Joseph. 1985. "Informational Structure of the Firm." *American Economic Review* 75, no. 2: pp. 303-307.

Arrow, Kenneth Joseph. 1985. "The Economics of Agency." In *Principals and Agents: The Structure of Business,* edited by John Winsor Pratt, and Richard Zeckhauser. Boston: Harvard Business School Press.

Attali, Jacques. 1978. *Rumori. Saggio sull'economia politica della musica.* Milan: Mazzotta.

Baumol, William J, and Wallace Oates. 1975. *The Theory of Environmental Protection.* Prentice-Hall: Englewood Cliffs.

Baumol, William J., and William G. Bowen. 1966. *Performing Arts: The Economic Dilemma. A Study of Problem Common to Theater.* New York: The Twentieth Century Fund.

Behhamou, Françoise. 2001. *L'economia della cultura.* Bologna: Il Mulino.

Bondardo Comunicazione. 2000. *Porta lontano investire in cultura: l'opinione degli italiani sul rapporto impresa-cultura.* Milan: Il sole 24 ore.

Brennan, Geoffrey, and James Buchanan. 1990. *La ragione delle regole.* Milan: F. Angeli.

Brosio, Giorgio. 1998. *Economia e finanza pubblica.* Rome: Carocci.

Bucci, Alberto, Paolo Figini and Massimiliano Castellani. 2003. "L'investimento in sponsorizzazione delle imprese. Un'analisi economica in termini statici e dinamici." *Rivista di politica economica* 93, no. 3: pp. 183-224.

Caves, Richard E. 2001. *L'industria della creatività. Economia delle attività artistiche e culturali.* Milan: Etas.

Chiacone, Aldo, and Franco Osculati. 1993. *Il merito della spesa pubblica. La natura e l'offerta dei beni non di mercato.* Milan: F. Angeli.

Cowen, Tyler, ed. 1988. *The Theory of market failure: a critical examination.* Fairfax: G. Mason University Press.

Curzi, Valter. 2004. *Bene culturale e pubblica utilità: politiche di tutela a Roma tra Ancien Règime e restaurazione.* Bologna: Minerva.

De Giorgi, Maria V. 1988. *Sponsorizzazioni e mecenatismo.* Padova: CEDAM.

De Sanctis, Velia. 2006. *Le sponsorizzazioni: analisi di un fenomeno.* Naples: Liguori.

Dell'Orso, Silvia. 2002. *Altro che musei: la questione dei beni culturali in Italia.* Bari: Laterza.

Di Maio, Amedeo. 1999. *Economia dei beni e delle attività culturali.* Naples: Liguori editore.

Eisenberg, Evan. 1997. *L'angelo con il fonografo: musica, dischi e cultura da Aristotele a Zappa.* Turin: Instar.

Forte, Francesco. 1993. "I beni meritori: scelte razioneli e supernazionali, esternalità, paternalismo, preferenze sulle preferenze." In *Il merito della spesa pubblica. La natura e l'offerta dei beni non di mercato,* edited by Aldo Chiacone, and Franco Osculati. Milan: F. Angeli.

Frey, Bruno, and Werner Pommerehne. 1991. *Muse e mercati. Indagine sull'economia dell'arte.* Bologna: Il Mulino.

Frey, Bruno. 2000. *Arts and Economics.* Berlin: Springer.

Frignani, Aldo, Anna Dassi, and Massimo Introvigne. 1993. *Sponsorizzazione merchandising pubblicità.* Turin: UTET.

Gravelle, Hugh, and Ray Rees. 1981. *Microeconomics.* London: Longman.

Graziani, Pietro, et al. 1992. *Il restauro tra mecenatismo e sponsorizzazioni: manuale per gli interventi d'architettura.* Rome: Bonsignori.

Hamilton, Barton. 2000. "Does Entrepreneurship Pay? An Empirical Analysis of Returns to Self-Employment." *Journal of Political Economy* 108, no. 3: pp. 604-631. [doi: 10.1086/262131]

Hansmann, Henry. 1981. "Nonprofit Enterprise in the Performing Arts." *Bell Journal of Economics* 12, no. 2: pp. 341-361.

Hare, Richard M. 1984. "Teoria etica e utilitarismo." In *Utilitarismo e oltre,* edited by Amartya Sen, and Bernard Williams. Milan: il Saggiatore.

Hauser, Andreas. 1953. *Sozialgeschichte der Kunst und Literatur.* München: C.H. Beck.

Hausman, Daniel, and Michael McPherson. 1993. "Taking Ethics Seriously: Economics and Contemporary Moral Philosophy." *Journal of Economic Literature* 31, no. 2: pp. 671-731.

Hodgson, Geoffrey M. 1988. *Economics and Institutions. A Manifesto for a Modern Institutional Economics.* Oxford: Polity Press-Basil Blackwell.

Keynes, John M. 1936. "Art and the State." In *The Collective Writings of John Maynard Keynes,* edited by Donald Moggridge. London: Macmillan-Cambridge University Press.

Keynes, John M. 1945. "The Arts Council. Its Policy and Scopes." In *The Collected Writings of John Maynard Keynes,* edited by Donald Moggridge. London: Macmillan-Cambridge University Press.

Krashinsky, Michael. 1986. "Transaction Costs and a Theory of Nonprofit Organization." In *The Economics of Nonprofit Institutions: Studies in Structure and Policy,* edited by Susan Rose Ackerman. Oxford: Oxford University Press.

Lambertini, Luca, and Raimondello Orsini. 1988. *Monopoly, quality, and network externalities.* Bologna: Università degli Studi di Bologna.

Liakopoulou, Irini. 2009. *Externality and merit goods: the case of cultural heritage.* Naples: Scriptaweb.

Lin, Steven. 1976. *Theory and measurement of economic externalities.* New York: Academic Press.

Luciani, Nino. 1992. *Economia delle scelte pubbliche di beni e servizi,* Milan: F. Angeli.

Lux, Simonetta. 1973. *Arte e industria,* Florence: Sansoni.

Magarotto, Luigi. 1980. *La letteratura irreale: saggio sulle origini del realismo socialista.* Venice: Marsilio.

Manacorda, Guido. 1942. *Il bolscevismo: marxismo, mistica, meccanesimo, ateismo, morale, politica, guerra, economia, letteratura e arte, scuola e propaganda.* Florence: G.C. Sansoni.

McManus, John. 1975. "The Costs of Alternative Economic Organisations." *Canadian Journal of Economics* 8, no. 3: pp. 334-350.

Musgrave, Richard A. 1987. "Merit Goods." In *The New Palgrave's Dictionary of Economics,* edited by John Eatwell, Murray Milgate, and Peter Newman. New York: Stockton Press.

Musgrave, Richard Abel. 1959. *The Theory of Public Finance.* New York: McGraw-Hill.

Onofri, Laura. 2003. "I contratti di sponsorizzazione. Un approccio Law and Economics." *Rivista di politica economica* 93, no. 3: pp. 225-252.

Pareto, Vilfredo. 1906. *Manuale di Economia politica.* Milan: Società Editrice Libraria.

Parfit, Derek. 1989. *Ragione e Persone.* Milan: Il Saggiatore.

Peacock, Alan, and Ilde Rizzo. 1994. *Cultural Economics and Cultural Policies.* London: Kluwer Academic Publishers.

Randon, Emanuela. 2002. *L'analisi positiva dell'esternalità: rassegna della letteratura e nuovi spunti.* Milan: Università degli Studi di Milano-Bicocca.

Robbins, Lionel. 1963. *Art and the State, Politics and Economics. Paper in Political Economy.* London: McMillan.

Rose-Ackerman, Susan. 1986. *The Economics of Non Profit Institutions: Studies in Structure and Policy.* Oxford: Oxford University Press.

Rosen, Sherwin. 1981. "The Economics of Superstars." *American Economic Review* 71, no. 5: 845-858.

Sen, Amartya. 1986. *Scelta, benessere, equità.* Bologna: Il Mulino.

Stiglitz, Joseph Eugene. 1988. *Economics of the Public Sector.* New York: Norton & Co.

Tellarini, Greta. 1997. "Il rapporto di sponsorizzazione: le esperienze italiana e spagnola a confronto." *Responsabilità comunicazione impresa* 2, no. 4: pp. 623-688.

Tirelli, Mario. 2005. *Politica economica e fallimenti di mercato: appunti di lezioni.* Rome: Aracne.

Tittmuss, Richard. 1963. *Essays on the Welfare State.* London: Allen Unwin.

Trimarchi, Michele. 1990. "Informazione, fiducia e reputazione nella struttura e nel finanziamento delle istituzioni culturali." In *Impresa pubblica, privatizzazione e regolamentazione,* edited by Emilio Giardina. Milan: Franco Angeli.

Trimarchi, Michele. 1993. *Economia e cultura. Organizzazione e finanziamento delle istituzioni culturali.* Milan: Franco Angeli.

Tullock, Gordon. 1997. *Economics of Income Redistribution.* Boston: Kluwer Academic Publishers.

Chapter 4

Art Market and Conceptual Marketing

Vladan Kuzmanovic

Belgrade University, Belgrade, Serbia

Abstract

Commodity and price are concepts of new border discipline – marginal or border marketing. Non-market act, non-price mass distribution, mass distribution from non-marketing to para-marketing activities, etc. Marketing is everything except what is not marketing. Non-marketing is marketing, where marketing is used as a relational phenomenon. As Baudrillard suggests, consumption is increasingly becoming a productive process, goal-oriented, and purposeful; furthermore, it requires that individuals be educated to carry out this process. In customizing oneself to (re)present marketable (self-)images, the consumer is interacting with other objects in the market to produce oneself, to purposefully position oneself. In this production process of the self-image(s) the consumer also acts as the marketer of self, selecting to use and interact with different other products that fit and enhance the image to be cultivated in each situation.

Marketing is everything related to marketing. Marketing is ancillary activities and para-activities: cultural marketing, market art, concepts of markets, market habits, market ambiences and market acts. At the beginning of the century, an interesting approach to freakonomics emerged for everything that it produced as a by-product of economics. Furthermore, with the development of marketing, a whole series of marginal disciplines and marginal concepts emerged. Instead of a multidisciplinary managerial approach, transdisciplinary phenomena come forth, e.g., between market art and marketing art, or marketing concept and market concept, etc.

Keywords: Art economics; art; conceptual markets; economic theories of art; marketing.

* * *

1. Introduction

Marketing is everything related to marketing. Marketing is ancillary activities and para-activities: cultural marketing, market art, concepts of markets, market habits, market ambiances and market acts (Janssen 2001). At the beginning of the century, an interesting approach to freakonomics emerged for everything that is produced as a by-product of economics. Economics is the whole complex, not only the focus—economics is at the very least a civilizational culture (economic, behavioral culture) and not just a social phenomenon, a set of social activities (Eun Park et al. 2010; Turley and Milliman 2000; Wang 2003). Furthermore, with the development of marketing, a whole series of marginal disciplines and marginal concepts emerged. Instead of a multidisciplinary managerial approach, transdisciplinary phenomena come forth, e.g., between market art and marketing act, or marketing concept and market concept, etc. Conceptual marketing, in this case, refers to much more than a marketing concept—it is a concept of marketing, and, namely, conceptual marketing. By "conceptual marketing," I mean a conceptual act or conceptual activity as a border category.

Once the price as a market activity is formed or tendered as a conceptual act, it is by all means under a market price. The price act refers to price as a conceptual, experimental value. Price is a concept or attitude. An actor is a bidder or price creator. Price is a product—price is for a product on offer; price is a concept. In a series of non-artistic topics, economic objects occur: brands, logos, labels, articles, commodities (Wang 2003). The basis of pop art is an economic phenomenon—consumerism. Artecon is everything from mass design to high art. Furthermore, art becomes a design concept instead of an expandable design.

2. Total Marketing and Complex Product

Design and price are concepts of new border discipline—marginal or border marketing. Non-market act, non-price mass distribution, mass distribution from non-marketing to paramarketing activities, etc. Marketing is everything except what is not marketing. Non-marketing is marketing, where marketing is used as a relational phenomenon. As Baudrillard (1988) suggests, consumption is increasingly becoming a productive process, goal-oriented, and purposeful; furthermore, it requires that individuals be educated to carry out this process. In customizing oneself to (re)present marketable (self-)images, the consumer is interacting with other objects in the market to produce oneself, to purposefully position oneself. In this production process of the self-image(s) `the consumer also acts as the marketer of self, selecting to use and interact with different other products that fit and enhance the image to be cultivated in each situation. Paramarketing encompasses a whole range of para-marketing activities that do not constitute mainstream marketing yet are closely related to the marketing culture (Firat et al. 1995). Paramarketing is a consumer-mediated activity and refers to the immediate experience of (co) lateral market experiences. Paramarketing is a set of para-activities. Para-marketing is a consumer-mediated activity; marketing itself is seen from the consumer's point of view as an object of the offer. The role of marketing in contemporary culture can best be understood by placing it into the system of exo/esomodernities. The market, and marketing as its institutionalized set of practices, has become a key institution of modern culture. Marketing does not create a concept/consumption, but a concept that is also an object of consumption.

Marketing is a system, a value, a complex. Marketing is a behavioral, interpersonal, and cultural concept (Wang 2003). The value of total marketing is the value of the exchange of signs, labels, recognition, identity, trends, time and comfort (Baudrillard 1988; Ogilvy 1990). Marketing consists of a set of brands, labels, logos, cultural patterns, communicative processes and interpersonal relationships. The complex product represents the overall marketing effect, not just the economic, segmental, targeted or lateral effects of marketing.

Total marketing is a set of activities related to a complex product and involves planning, creating, conceiving, registering and reusing complex products. It involves revaluation, interaction, and an enhancement of utility in a progressive marketing system.

3. Conceptual marketing

Marketing itself can be a need, in addition to dealing with needs. The mediation of marketing—as a subject of marketing itself—can help reframe the market and the overall social effect of marketing. In addition to the basic goal—finding the need—, marketing also generates other goals, which are generally oriented to increasing customer convenience through a marketing environment or a set of referral values.

Total marketing includes basic, extended and referral marketing, which recalibrates conventional marketing by resetting the entire process as a new process offering. Classical marketing referral is about activity correction. The use of marketing as a form is represented through conceptual marketing: once realized, the marketing process becomes a form that can be sold, changed, and offered.

Contextual markets are complexes that are remarketed in different iterative contexts and under different circumstances. A seller brings to the market a holistic system, the whole complex not just a part or process. Conceptual marketing deals with holistic entities, and a context product is a marketing entity. Customer perception is a meta-narrative. The buyer also needs market reminiscences. The product complex includes the basic, extended, and external product (Figure 4.1).

It seems that postmodernism is no longer a theory or a philosophical stance but a reality which impacts many facets of life, specifically in Western societies. It is represented in world views which are increasingly becoming prominent, and also in the conditions such as, hyperreality, fragmentation, decentring of the subject, reversal of production and consumption, paradoxical juxtaposition of opposites, and non-commitment to meta-narratives. An external product is referred to by the position and interaction of the product in a marketing environment. The marketing environment is the practice of the customer to value non-economic phenomena as economic according to their market experience, habits, profile attitude, or feelings. The external product primarily involves a large number of paramarketing activities as consumer habits and behavioral processes. To illustrate this, just a few examples of hobby marketing activities and the hippie marketing subculture. The phenomenon of fanecons began in the early 1970s in America. Antimarketing, anti-shopping and a whole host of deviant three-way behaviors originated in response to consumerist culture (Barksdale and Darden 1972; Kangun et al. 1975; Firat 1992).

In some Western countries, buying is seen as a ritual—even more, as a cult—and the buying process itself is implemented as a performance, a subversion, or a sentimental act. The buyer is proactive or deactive; the buyer does not only delay specific marketing messages or incentives (Aaker and Day 1982; d'Astous et al. 1990). Purpose–innovative consumers are an important market segment (Youn and Faber 2000; Bellenger and Korgaonkar 1980). Para-shopping is an activity of buying irrelevant, unnecessary and unwanted things, shopping out of the mainstream, deliberately buying non-advertised goods, including superficial and collateral shopping, with a selection of less desirable and less important items as an act. The concept of the recreational shopper identity, a dimension of the consumer's self-concept, is contrasted with simple shopping enjoyment, which has characterized most past research on recreational shopping. Recreational shopping enthusiasts are found to engage more extensively in a range of retail shopping behaviors to spend more money shopping (i.e., they are not just browsers), and are more "multi-channel" than other shoppers (Reynolds et al. 2002; Guiry et al. 2006).

A collected object becomes a reminder of the story of its acquisition. The object is, thus, a cue for recalling and retelling this story. The images that a collection conjures up may therefore be a part of the collector's personal history of times and places. Stewart calls these associations "souvenirs" (because of their metonymic authentication of the past) and distinguishes them from collections (which she contends involve only a metaphoric derivation of authenticity from the past). However, we consider personal history to be an inescapable part of collections: "It is as if the experience of possession could be transformed into the possession of experience" (Belk et al. 1991).

Affiliate marketing takes place between the buyer and the seller, the result is a surefire effect, greater than expected, in deact or proact, irrational rationality, dynamic marketing relationship, a recognizable affect versus effect. The customer subjectively responds to objective influences. The buyer is creative, which means that he does not only respond formally to marketing stimuli. Objective influences always expect objective reactions; however, reactions are subjective and behavioral. The solution to this is in subjective stimuli in a one-to-one project relationship.

3.1. Fanecon

Fanecons have, in some sense, made a mark in marketing culture with the advent of hippie culture and consumerism branding and marketing expansion in the 70s. Fanecon binds to specific brand products or is experimenting with brands. Fanecon is a sub-cultural consumer. Fanecon is a consumer of the time market. And, why not, fanecon is a proactive consumer (Kotler 1977; Belk et al. 1991).

Brand culture refers to the cultural influences and implications of brands in two ways. First, we live in a branded world: brands infuse culture with meaning, and brand management exerts a profound influence on contemporary society. Brand culture represents one interdisciplinary framework for understanding how brands create value and meaning. Second, brand culture provides the third leg for brand theory—in conjunction with brand identity and brand image, brand culture provides the necessary cultural, historical and political grounding to understand brands in context. Future consumer research on visual issues must acknowledge images' representational and rhetorical power both as cultural artefacts and as engaging and deceptive bearers of meaning, reflecting broad societal, cultural, and ideological codes (Beatty and Ferrell 1998; Youn and Faber 2000). A brand community is a specialized bound community based on a structured set of social relations among admirers of a brand. Muniz and O'Guinn (2001) use ethnographic and computer-mediated environment data to explore the characteristics, processes, and particularities of three brand communities (those centered on Ford Bronco, Macintosh, and Saab). These brand communities exhibit three traditional markers of community: shared consciousness, rituals and traditions, and a sense of moral responsibility.

Economics is not a disciplinary approach, but a disciplinary fundability instead. Discipline is in this new order of things, a concept, not projection but output, effectuation. Instead of bijection, there is an inversion of concepts, instead of a variable concept, a concept-variable (price concept/concept price, design concept/concept design, market concept/concept-market, marketing concept/conceptual marketing, act concept/concept activity). Conceptual marketing consists of concepts that are not aspects but economic projects; each discipline is a concept or project—behavioral, psychological, cultural, communicative, etc. (Schroeder 2008).

Marketing is ultimately conceived as an economic project toward everything. Marketing is an economic project. The set goals are not projections (as in the classical scheme) but projects. This means that activities are viewed by individuals as their own capabilities; they do not mediate them but rather recognize them. Activities are an internal set of goals and activities effectuated by individuals. In a firm, activity is understood as a project, and the individual is motivated to accomplish the task. If he accomplishes it, he is realized not only as an employee, but also as a personality. A personality has far greater potential than non-personality as an employee.

The design of the object neglects the ergonomic and develops the conceptual side. The questions of what the usable value of a non-object is and which attributes of the design are ergonomic arise, as well as the practical understanding. Design is the concept of activity or non-action, applied art to the design of a non-object. Usefulness refers to the effect—the benefit of the object in this case—the object has as conceptual applications, so it is possible to dispute the pre-conceptual and applied design of any such objects. In the case of a modern object, artists talk about the design of the concept. Modern art replaces the concept of design with the design of the concept. The object is designed from the utility of benefit or benefits (Denicola 1983).

For an individual, the real aesthetic effect is beneficial. The object produces an effect. The consumption of an object is the consumption of a specific context in relation to objects. The concept is an ambiance or relation-convenience. The object is an activity related to the object. In this sense, the design is a project of contextual activities. The object exists only in interaction. Design is the concept of usable interactions. Concept-design, therefore, refers to non-objects, sculpture is non-dimensional. Design is an activity of an effect or benefit. Concept designs the context of the object. The object has an aesthetic effect even in the contingent of its absence. The object is an aesthetic position or reconstruction. This position is the position of a value system or effect.

Design is the concept of the object. The object is everything, even a non-object, mental image, the concept has more with the nature of this effect and not with an object that by definition can be a non-object, non-existent or underart.

Instead of a meta-object, we deal with a real act, a conceptual object, a target effect, a single conceptual act, or a non-activity. Finally, active design, or activities toward non-activities. Especially interesting is the transition from meta-narrative, deconstruction, concept of art, dadaism to anamodernism and conceptual performance, conceptual literature, post-experiment and super-narrative. Art is an extensive meta-narrative. Literature is a continuous act. It comes to the mixing of art, first of all performative and fictional genres. The context is most perceptible in the absence of text. Structurism is inter-genre context.

Conceptual art has made quite progression from Malevich's White on White (1916) canvas to Luba's Blank Canvas (2019) and non-tangible objectivity.

Significant attention is given to the forms of anamodernism expressed with the series of Luba's works: Pistol (2018), One (2018), Blank Canvas (2019), as well as through conceptual literature. The "Pistol" is a great representative of anti-object art.

Superlatives with new possible readings: the most expensive non-object, the most expensive object, as well as a number of parametric experiments that extensify specific quantitive properties of objects. Non-tangible object and non-tangible art is the basis of a new sculptural expression. The acquits of experiment, deconstruction, conceptual art and neo-dada, its response found in anamodernity, neo-experiment, and new concept. The superistic tendencies of supramatism, zenithism, neo-expressionism, neo-Dadaism its perpetuations certainly found in tensurrealism and a whole series of isms. Useful outlets of superflat, stuckism, intervention, interactive art and new media art (Cham 2006).

Finally, the design allows pure art reading, in the conceptual activity the object is not subordinate. Design is not a rigid form, but an aesthetic effect.

A pure or new object is an object deprived of any prejudice about that and only that specific object, the object is anything that can stand in the perception or imagination of the viewer.

The object is in the position of consciousness, in the dimension of the context. A pure object is an activity oriented towards the effect or interpretation. Interpretation depends on the pre-context (system of values), the art system, and the context, that is, the position of the object, as the non-exhibit, and tendency of the object.

4. Art Systems vs. Systems of Art

However, the main focus of modernism is direct relationship, direct art, direct contemporary art. In this sense, art is the radicalization of modernity, the immediate experience of reality. Immediacy is its originality, first of all in theoretical development we should plead the synthetic principle, proactive art, avant-garde method, complementarity, system, ambiguity. The budget of modernity does not exist, it is not diminished but is enlarged, according to the progression of facts and diversification (Rancière 2014; Smith 2006).

In this sense, theories, and not just modern theories (as in case of postmodernism), are systems and should be treated as systems. In anamodernism, theory, an element, is possibility, disponibility, choice. Furthermore, there are no modernity budgets.

The question is not what could be contemporary, but what is contemporary. Less attention should be paid to post-modernity, as post-modernism pays attention to modernism.

Basically, modernism is a binary reaction, and post-modernism is a polyreaction. The theories are bilateral and multilateral controversies. Instead of ejections, it is necessary to talk about synthesis, it is necessary to introduce polylateral synthesis at the place of bilateral ones. Let's not forget the arts are the system and, as such, they are multifaceted relations. Anamodernism insists on a polyvalent synthesis of isms, more precisely in their introduction into a system of values, which as elements can be used and revalidated. These inter-territorial transfers, artistic transfers, happen individually, but not systemically. But for art to be a system, there are no exclusivities, there are systems, and there are exchanges, more or less homogeneous. Exchanges because art is continuity, nature, system. Means, procedures, format, and, to some extent, styles, are (re) validations of the art systems. [1]

Modernism has no exclusivity but a synthetic proclamation. If it creates art as a system, the system is exclusive. On the other hand, the exclusivity problem is a theoretical problem not an artistic.

If there was no theory, art would not doubt. Art works in the medium, and intermodally. Theory is intermodal, theory is the concept of art. The concept versus art, but the concept through art, the concept in art, the concept is articulated through art, it does not define art, but itself is created through art, not intramodally, but intermodally, not as an artifice of attitudes, theory of theories.

---

[1] The value of the system is reflected in its contribution to the overall system as new possibilities for modernity, and hence to the individual system.

Actual art is a concept, non-actual concept is an imposition, the avant-garde does not have this problem. The avant-garde is nonchalant and actual. The avant-garde is contemporary to the experience of art. The avant-garde is actuality and every actuality is an immediate art. The concept is intertemporality in time. As we can see, the concept serves to develop a sustainable contemporaneity. Whether modernity is real or temporary art, is actual art also contemporary art is contemporary art also permanent art, how to preserve modernity in temporal connotation, without concept? That is, how to interpret a concept as a possibility or an experiment, as an element or a connotative means, as a timestamp. A connotative non-timestamp should be introduced. Beauty is a complementary value. Art is quality.

The avant-garde is immediate, non-invasive. Neofluxus, neodada, stuckism, experiment art, are noncontinuous, usable concepts. The avant-garde is a connotation, every act here is a connotative value.

The whole series of avant-garde movements do not signify, and yet their concepts are reconnotation.

If anything L.H.O.O.Q. (1919) is a more blatant attack on traditional values than Fountain. Duchamp has taken one of the most celebrated masterpieces of European art – the Mona Lisa – and defaced it. By adding a goatee and moustache, he has turned the enigma into an androgyne and underscored the point with an obscene play on words. When the letters are read phonetically in French they sound like the sentence: "Elle a chaud au cul" (she has a hot arse). Commenting on his motives, Duchamp said: "In 1919, when Dada was in full blast, and we were demolishing many things, the Mona Lisa became a prime victim. I put a moustache and a goatee on her face simply with the idea of desecrating it" (Schwarz 1997). The readymade, then, rejects the values supremely associated with the Mona Lisa and by turning it into an obscene image is primarily intended to disreward aesthetic contemplation. It gives expression to a profound nihilism. The readymades influenced later generations of artists, including Joseph Kosuth and the Conceptualists, many of whom wished to abolish the object partly, among other things, in order to resist the commodification of art and partly to purge art of aesthetics and demonstrate how it could enjoy an independent existence. The Conceptual Art movement, then, appropriates anti-art for its own strategic purposes.

The point is this: aesthetics, as we have pointed out, are conceptually irrelevant to art. Thus, any physical thing can become objet d'art, that is to say, can be considered tasteful, aesthetically pleasing, etc. But this has no bearing on the object's application to an art context; that is, its functioning in an art context. (I.e., if a collector takes a painting, attaches legs, and uses it as a dining table it's an act unrelated to art or the artist because, as art, that wasn't the artist's intention) (Humble 2002).

Art has to learn a lot from these itemporal modernities. How something contemporary remains intertemporal as a concept, and why that concept is reusable. Why Fluxus is the actual method, and why its act is renewingly reconnotative. The bids here are more than desirable, and not theoretical, though they are concepts. Answer: the reason is because the concept here is an act, and not invasive, non-connotative, contemporary. Neofluxus is an art concept.

Anamodernity is an act of reality, a real paradigm, an act-concept, not a pre-concept. Anamodernity occurs, like, interaction, extension. Art is a vanguard need, a necessity for contemporary and original reality, for a new act of new reality, the concept of direct experience, for act-transfer, transfer of real art (art-reality), for development from a controversy to a complex.

From the system of controversy to the absurd, from the problem of the absurd to the problem of modernity. However, to resolve the issue of natural art means to set it to achieve pure civilizational value.

5. The Starting Position of Modernity Is Somewhat Difficult

The "value" of particular artists after Duchamp can be weighed according to how much they questioned the nature of art; which is another way of saying "what they added to the conception of art" or what wasn't there before they started. Artists question the nature of art by presenting new propositions as to art's nature. And to do this one cannot concern oneself with the handed-down "language" of traditional art, as this activity is based on the assumption that there is only one way of framing art propositions. But the very stuff of art is indeed greatly related to "creating" new propositions. The case is often made – particularly in reference to Duchamp – that objects of art (such as the Ready-mades, of course, but all art is implied in this) are judged as objets d'art in later years and the artists' intentions become irrelevant. Such an argument is the case of a preconceived notion ordering together not necessarily related facts (Kosuth 1991).

Conceptual art might be considered as work that emphasized the underlying conditions of aesthetic experience: Language was seen as foremost among these conditions. Material form and sensory perception were made secondary to analyses of their discursive and institutional frames. (Ward 1997; Morgan 1994) The question is whether the concept can be proactive except in the present, every other activity is projection - that is, pre-conceptualization. The possibilities of the concept in the present are great. The concept is active modernity.

In the new, anamodernist tendencies, the contextualization of art, the contextualization of acts and processes, the tendency that emerged in performance and interactive art (i.e., active performance then participatory performance) its reliable affirmation found in relational art, which has transformed this multi-ferential, in collaboration with installation, instructional art, place art, public media art, turned into one complex relationship (Bourriaud 2002; Sharp et al. 2005; Vermeulen and Akker 2014).

Development of art, out-institutional, out-of-place, transitive, non-conformist. Or in the example of an adverse act of nonexhibit, a non-arbitrated act, a parallel and a counter-act, an out-exhibit that can only derive its meaning from a non-exhibit, non-event, event, etc.

The problematic nature of anti-art is best illustrated by a crucial but ambiguous question, which Duchamp jotted down in 1913 when he was in the midst of an artistic crisis. That question was: "Can one make works which are not works of art?" It can be interpreted in at least three different ways. The first interpretation takes into account Duchamp's dismissal of Modernism as so-called "retinal" art, i.e. art that placed painterly, formal values before ideas. Thus the question could be formulated as: is it possible to make works that are not "retinal" works of art but which embody a broader aesthetic? The second interpretation is more radical: is it possible to make works that eschew the aesthetic altogether and are the antithesis of art? The third interpretation gives the question a very different inflection: is it possible for Duchamp to make works that would not, inevitably, be named as art, i.e. could be anything other than art? It is hardly surprising, then, that the work Duchamp went on to produce between 1913 and 1923 is a mixed bag, and contains both art and anti-art in the strict sense (Humble 2002).

Cray argues that we should reconsider the role of the supposedly "dematerialized" object. Schellekens is friendly to this suggestion, stating that "we should be wary of the conceptualist's claim that the focus of appreciation in conceptual art does exclude the [means] completely and art."

To Leung conceptual artworks, then, should be identified neither with ideas themselves nor with fusions of ideas and artifacts nor with sets of such things. He proposes instead that conceptual artworks are imbued artifacts. They are physical objects, events, activities, or perhaps tokens of some other type of object—perhaps even ideas!—that stands in a special relation to certain ideas (Leung 2007).

In Big Torn Campbell's Soup Can the spectacular applique is literally alienated from its referent, but even in the untouched soup cans, this alienation is conveyed through the complete engulfment of the product by its packaging. Pop art is founded in such dualities in which Campbell's soup, for example, may simultaneously circulate as an image of American family values within the spectacular economy of the media and as an inexpensive processed foodstuff on the shelves of every supermarket. Just as Warhol's EPI dramatized a model of subjectivity in which kinesthetic experience is always on the verge of transforming into mediated experience, his model of objectivity developed years earlier, established an analogous alternating current between the commodity as a representation and the commodity as a use-value (Joselit 2002; Kunzle 1984).

6. Conceptual Market

Conceptual marketing studies the concepts and uses of generic marketing values, concepts and marking of consumer values. A dynamic image is a set of active values. The market consists of a product market and a perception market, even with the fact that the market is fixed, the product perception market is still dynamic.

These are synthetic markets, complementary value sets. The incremental set is augmented by the values of the previous set. The concept is a system of complementary values.

The conceptual market is a model of the market that offers a concept to meet the expressed need. A concept is a form of satisfying a need. The concept is the stated request or perception. The concept is consumer perception, be it image, idea, aspect or use. The product does not need to exist, nor does the market object. The market is about redefining, reformulating, reusing the market for existing products and active systems.

Commodity, the subject of the conceptual market is of non-tangible value. The conceptual market is demand remarketing. Process value is the transfer or ratio of aligned needs, benefits and costs. The conceptual process involves recalibrating and remarketing all elements of the market and supply.

The conceptual market is a process of market recalibration, the goal of marketing is supplying demand. Marketing describes integration (focus) and calibration (refocus). In that sense, market supply can be anything, even the very way in which an object is perceived or offered. The object of the conceptual market is only that market over different periods of time, therefore, it speaks of quoting needs, forms as requirements to meet needs, while the object, generic need, is the same however form, ways of meeting needs differ (Aaker and Day 1982).

The conceptual market is the analysis of abstract, non-tangible, interactive value, such as assumption, assessment, belief, subjective value. The context of the conceptual market thus relativizes the notion of economic variables by putting them in the same interactive relationship.

However, prices are not fixed but active sets. From a demand standpoint, the concept is any value that can be marketed.

Conceptual markets are art markets with pronounced economic variables (Campbell 2008; Courty and Pagliero 2014).

The art market in a contemporary position is characterized by a supply of value, where supply is a concept or market value. The market offers a concept that has value as such, that is as a conceptual act, for the seller, the relation of value as a concept is relativized by the act of supply - the conceptual act. The concept remarkets value to the consumer and the consumer accepts/evaluates the offer as a conceptual product (Kangun et al. 1975). In concept, the seller is the consumer, the consumer is the interpreter and seller. The consumer determines the price himself. Art markets are specific markets with both side actors, consumer interpretation, conceptual act and interactive process. The concept is a general category, an act, a concept can equally be the concept of free purchases or of overpricing buying. The collector expresses his desire to pay more for the work than it costs, through the marketing of exclusive purchases, as a conceptual act of purchase and the concept of an impossible price, etc.

A concept is a marketing idea or form that is realized through a set of offers, through marketing and sales. The artistic concept, the concept of art markets is defined as a set of non-exclusive, non-economic values. The conceptual art market is defined by offering a variety of values (real and fixed sets). It is also worth the specific rule that supply (both price and quantity) is always higher than demand. Although supply is higher than demand, this does not lead to a fall in the prices at the art market, because supply is not substantive and good products are of unique value. Higher supply than demand actually fixes prices at a higher level. This is the effect of the conceptual price, in general, the supply will always be higher than the demand, and the offered price will always be higher, rarely lower than the seeking price, nevertheless, the purchases will be made as conceptually effective acts.

Remarketing and conceptualization are the two basic tools of modern marketing. Conceptualizing uses in contextual circumstances. The company's core business is to *sell mark* to contextual markets.

Figure 4.1 | Theories of the Art Market

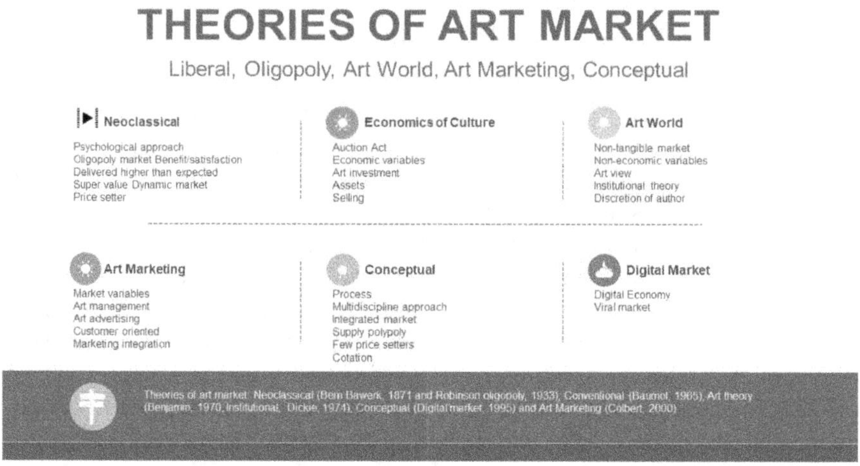

Neoclassical, Art World, Institutional, Conceptual, Digital Market and Art Marketing. (Baumol 1965, Benjamin 1970, Dickie 1975, Evard and Cobert 2000)

Remarketing is the integration of elements towards customer-driven value. Integration of functions and elements into the overall image. In other words, the marketing function is valued both internally and externally (integral marketing and market integration). Marketing integrates all functions, and marketing itself is integrated with market function.

Marketing generates effects and values that are perceived differently. The temporal way of perceiving an image is a dynamic image. Each value is scaled dynamically as a market perception. Scalable marketing deals with dynamic image and its generating. Thus two marketing processes are perpetuated: value and positioning of value (remarketing and conceptualization) (Figure 4.3).

The art market and other markets are realized through conceptualization, through branding, activities, relation and use. Price is offered as a mark, a sale of a mark, as conceptual art and a concept art market. In the conceptual market, commodities are marks sales. These are concrete and realistic systems that are used daily in complex market interactions, and consumers have large discretionary thresholds, deciding iteratively, individually and autonomously (Grampp 1989). The complex model of increased consumer discretion and active decision-making assumes an enhanced dynamic model, in response to an interactive schematic market (Sagot-Duvauroux 2003).

Figure 4.2 | Art Markets Through Time

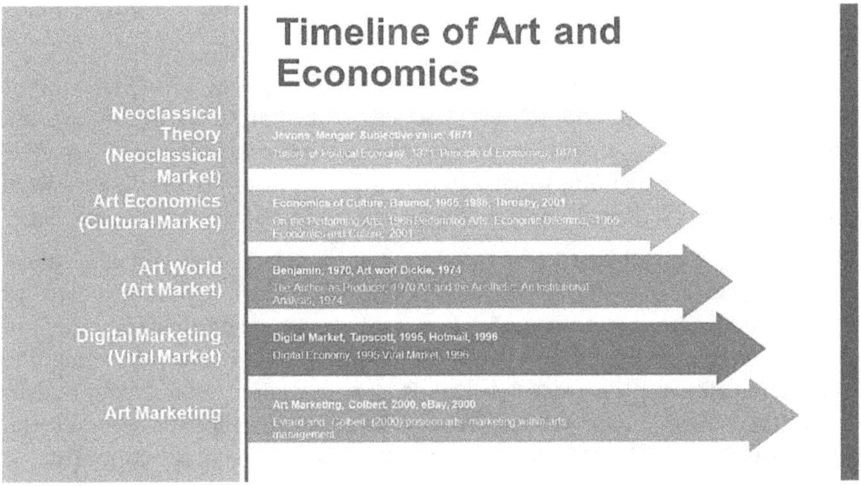

Art Markets through time: Neoclassical Market (1871), Cultural Market (1965), Culture of Economics and Art (2001), Art Market (1974), Digital Market (1995), Art Marketing (2000)

The digital market as an interactive market is the minimal definition of the conceptual market. The working approach describes the market in real-time, the relativization of the positions and arts. Discretion is maximal and emphasized, opportunities are considerable, demand is proactive, supply is plentiful, yet positions are mutual. The interactive market is characterized by a dynamic exchange of values and needs, innovative values and active demand. The innovative marketplace creates active demand. A digital market is a new form of real-time market. The art market as a concept of interactive buying and selling.

The digital market is an individual market for a conceptual market act. Private art is another example of an individual act.

Between the end of the twentieth century and the beginning of the twenty-first, art entered a new era – namely, an era of mass artistic production following an era of mass art consumption. Contemporary means of image production, such as video and cell phone cameras, as well as socially networked means of image distribution such as Facebook, YouTube, and Twitter, give global populations the possibility of presenting their photos, videos, and texts in a way that cannot be distinguished from any other post-conceptual artwork. And contemporary design gives the same populations the possibility of shaping and experiencing their own bodies, apartments, or workplaces as artistic objects and installations. This means that contemporary art has definitively become a mass cultural practice. Furthermore, it means that today's artist lives and works primarily among art producers – not among art consumers. Or, to use Greenberg's phrase, the artist is finally put squarely into the context of production.

The concept is "super content," therefore, something that is not just content but an approach to content, to the expected and desired value. In the case of a work of art, super content is recognizable because value greatly exceeds expected value by creating super-satisfaction. A work of art produces a wow effect; in a sense, it does not produce a neutral, indifferent or regular impact.

In the words of Stiglitz, the overarching argument is that "price serves a function in addition to that usually ascribed to it in economic theory: it conveys information and aspects behavior" (Mossetto 1993). In particular, prices are used to judge the quality of a good, or, to put it in other words, quality is "screened" utilizing the price level. This signaling effect is not confined to uninformed parties who lack other sources of information to estimate the quality of goods. Michael Spence, who was one of the first economists to recognize the relevance of signaling in markets, argued that sellers correlate the quality of goods within a product line with the price based on experience. As a result, price changes send quality signals to informed, frequent buyers of those goods (Velthuis 2003; 2004).

Velthuis (2003) argue that price setting is not just an economic but also a signifying act: despite their impersonal, businesslike connotations, actors on markets manage to express a range of cognitive and cultural meanings through prices. Previously, meanings of prices have been recognized in signaling theories within economics. However, these meanings are restricted to pro¢t opportunities.

Worldwide auction sales of postwar and contemporary art climbed to a historic peak of 4.9 billion euros, or $6.8 billion, a massive increase over the €1.42 billion in auction sales in 2009, according to the 2014 Art Market Report published by the European Fine Art Foundation in March.

They were also spending a lot of money on art. Exactly 100 years ago, the czar of Russia, Nicholas II, clearly mindful of the unrest being fomented by his downtrodden subjects, bought Leonardo da Vinci's "Benois Madonna" in a private transaction for $1.5 million. That Leonardo, priced at three times the record $500,000 paid by J. Pierpont Morgan for Raphael's "Colonna" altarpiece in 1901, was cited by the late Gerald Reitlinger in "The Economics of Taste" (1982) as probably the most expensive art sale in history, factoring in inflation (Reyburn 2014).

Figure 4.3 | Conmark Model

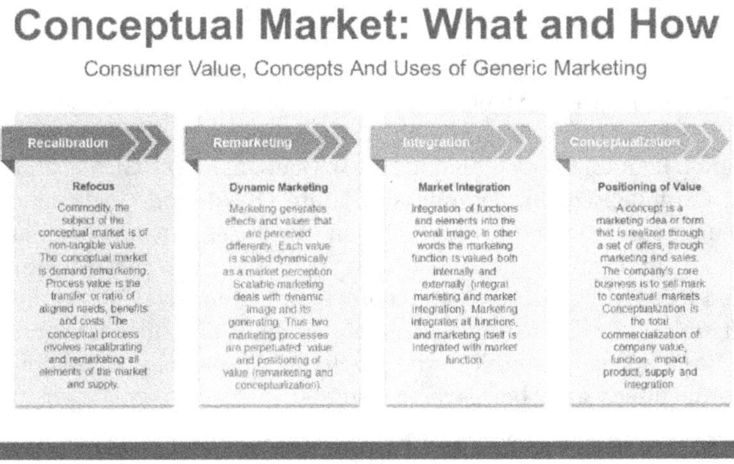

Four elements of conceptual marketing: (i) recalibration, (ii) remarketing, (iii) integration and (iv) conceptualization. From this, marketing processes are perpetuated: value and positioning of value (remarketing and conceptualization).

Two-sided approaches to art instead of the one-sided market, conceptual versus neoclassical and artistic approaches. The theories aim to soften the starting positions of both the economic and non-economic approaches of rigid negotiating positions as mild and scaled positions (Figure 4.1).

In the integrative approach, the negotiator is also the consumer; the roles are transferable. One should avoid the ultimate concepts that are expressed in sentences like "author against the market," "market against consumer." The actors are not opposed to each other but are in the same process of creating a mutual value—context.

The modern market is made from a new neoclassical and conceptual model—from a Robinson oligopoly and atomized structures, and the goal is to move to a conceptual and advanced market model (Figure 4.2). The contemporary market is a polypol of supply; it is global, interactive, and is characterized by fragmented demand and an excessive number of products. In general, the question is how the conventional model of the '70s is sustainable for the interactive market, the simultaneous and global market and polypol tend to crystallize new solutions which are already embodied in a multidisciplinary approach and dynamic settings, relativization of economic and non-economic variables, interactive consumer market process, etc.

The work of art is dynamic, interactive, mutual and processive.[2] The tendency of art markets is expressed through the transition from neoclassical oligopolies to conceptual polypolies.

Ever since Baumol's approach, efforts have been made to formulate the economics of art, with an emphasis on the business of the public sector. These tendencies are aimed at determining the price and auctioning the value on the art market. Baumol (1986), Pesando (1993), Goetzmann (1993), Mei and Moses (2002), Campbell (2008), Pesando and Shum (2008), and Goetzmann et al. (2011) have studied the price appreciation of art over time and compared the returns to those on financial assets. At the same time, the real process is adorned with a diffuse market and a process of interactive consumption and non-linear relations. The diffuse dynamic model is described by connotative uses, harmonized quantities and exchange protocols, quotations and conceptual prices, as - a barter value system.

The basic economic theories of the art market, neoclassical, conventional and conceptual, are based on economic, psychological and behavioral factors and analyze market decisions and microeconomic conditions in which individuals act. The conceptual theory makes no distinction between economic and non-economic variables and studies global, progressive, integrative and digital markets. New market forms and new processes require new theories. Neoclassical theory combined psychological factors such as individual and subjective values and the usefulness and satisfaction of the individual in relation to the product. Neoclassical theory is the first market theory of art and a kind of precursor to the market, consumer-oriented model.

The auction model studies market variables, including non-tangible values and market asset value movements. The conceptual (digital) model seeks to expand frame-work and relativize meanings in accordance with up-date conditions in active art markets.

7. Referral and Activity

In the 21st century, the relationship is understood as a concept. A work of art is not an object, but a multi-active variable, the ultimate product of experience, perception, presentation, publicity, interaction, positioning, a positive impression. A work of art is a synergy of all persons participating in the artistic process; on the other hand, the artistic process does not end with the creation, but with the perception, the effectuation of the work. Indeed, at least two or

---

[2] A work of art is actually a concept or result of a consumer process that is interpreted here as context or contextual use. A work of art is not a product but an interaction between individuals and the result of that interaction.

more persons are required for art. The work of art is in its full meaning all that is about the work; we can talk about the complex-work and its full effect. Publicity, recognition, attitude, popularity, perception, interpretation, accessibility, etc., are also included in this context (Cosmo 2019). A work of art is a synergy of relationships and experiences regarding the work. A relationship is a complex experience.

New media is everywhere in museums these days—in the form of hand-held information devices, installation art, display supports, and archiving systems, as a means to reorganize working practices and to keep track of visitors. It is used to make new kinds of museums, such as "virtual museums," and to represent the things in existing museums. Most simply described as computer-based or digital media, it is the product of the convergence of mass-media practices.

During record-breaking art auctions at Christie's and Sotheby's, the amount of money spent often exceeds the gross domestic product of small island nations. As an outsider, it's hard to see results like Christie's $745 million contemporary art auction in May of 2013 as anything other than a pissing contest of conspicuous consumption. Yet, insiders in the art market describe these purchases as investments (Mayyasi 2018).

Relational art draws the premise from marketing art, namely relationship-marketing art. The product is not an object of art but a variable process, relationship building, as further emphasized, is of importance too. Interaction has a long-lasting and mutual value; it is not the work that is produced but the interaction, not the means, but the effect.

Since the 1960s, an increasing number of artists have been taking active engagement further. Most famously, in the period of happenings, direct and physical audience participation became an integral part of the artwork or performance. Situations were set up by the artists in which the audience was meant to engage by actually taking part and so explicitly determine the work. The artwork itself is changed by the audience. Indeed, the activity of engagement became part of the artwork. Often with the help of electronics, members of the audience were able to touch artwork and cause it to change. Art became interactive.

The avant-garde of the 21st century is characterized by the mixing of movements, that is, the emergence of polyvalent art and theoretical polynomials, complex systems and semi-complex systems. In considering the necessity of avant-garde incentives, a striking mix of avant-garde and neo-avant-garde directions, in a new connotation, avant-garde and neo-avant-garde, the distinction between the various modernist efforts of (re) modernism is lost; or modernisms and postmodernisms, metamodernisms, neomodernisms

(Kostelanetz 2018; Moxey 2012). In this sense, there are specific connotations (revalidations) of the elements, that is, the art systems of these reconnotated values.

The values of the system are ambiguous, as they are reused (revalidated) or conceptualized inter-temporally. Their values are reduced, clear, explicit, non-theoretical, or solidly theoretical (core value). The avant-garde is the first system due to its multifaceted act. Avant-garde is an act. The concept of the avant-garde system is always modern. The avant-garde is attitude, principle, set of activities, set of performances, articulatory forms, positive objects and processes (MacRitchie 1996; Phelan 2004).

Because of its mediation, the avant-garde is non-devaluing, general-valid. The less theoretical explication and the more explicit artwork, the more explicit reality, hence the more explicit extravagant modernity. Extravagant art is the answer to explicit modernity. Spectacle and attraction, underart; detraction, ritual, pamphlet, deact. However, although a conceptual approach, the avant-garde is not an exploited or consumable set, but a concept act. Theory devalues art in the long run. Theory limits, art is a timeless sign. Dadaism is one of the most frequently revalidated art movements, and yet it is theoretically infinitesimally explained. Dadaism is a raw artistic act, an act without words. Reaction to reality, art that responds to reality. Yet we know so little about dadaism, though so much has been said. The act of avant-garde is in perception of reality.

The avant-garde is the negation of everything but modernity because the avant-garde is modernity. The avant-garde is both experiment and emotion; the hub and the absurd. Is an avant-garde tradition? Hard to say, but in the connotative sense, a connotation is a form for an act. The avant-garde is an excess or affirmative. The avant-garde is actual against the mainstream. The avant-garde has no problem with the absurd, as it faces real problems. Art as a philosophy often seeks to circumvent the problem of absurdity by rejecting it or by falling into it.

The problem of the absurdity of art is exclusivity, not synthesis. Absurdity is understood as a phenomenon, that is, exclusivity, it is exclusive or obsessive. However, absurd is the system, difficult to comprehend. Who understands the absurd will understand the reality. The system is a synthesis of absurdity and reality, against reality without the absurd (and reality with the absurd). That is why the absurd is included in the system.

Art ranges from the theoretical absurd to the absurd of theory; art is an antimodern model. However, absurdity contradicts modernist efforts, which is, after all, evident in the explications of the series of neo-modernisms. Art is an artificial non-modernism. Artificiality has been re-evaluated by being put out of modernity. However, the model is contemporary, and will always be contemporary, because it is modern. Its modernity will not be a problem, because it is in the system where all other values and arts are contemporary. From reality to the absurdity of the medium, from the model of the absurd to the absurd of the concept.

8. Concept

In non-figurative art, the emergence of non-exhibits occurs with the simultaneous revalidation of the boundary between figurative and fine art. The non-object of new conceptual art brings to the fore the problem of the medium. The medium does not have to exist as such for art to exist. What is more, the achievement of the new conceptual art informs us that the art of media exists without media as such. The medium is, therefore, a modality, a position, a human perception. Media is a concept and art is modal, yes, but since the new art of the 21st century, it seems that the activity or viewpoint of the artist is more important than the means or action (Cham 2006).

The art-work does not have to exist; for an artist to exist, the form does not have to exist, and even activity itself does not have to exist, activity, relation, and actor (the viewer, not the interpretation). Art is intermodal and non-objective. Or it is an intramodal deact. Non-exhibit is an immediate represent. Non-object non-anti-object of pre-contextual art. The arts are shaped by intellectual achievement and reflect the belief systems of a society. The modern culture industry deals with consumers' needs within industrial, political, economic and global settings (Horkheimer and Adorno 1972).

A contemporary interpretation of arts marketing should acknowledge its foundations in the application of the marketing mix, but it needs to move forward on its own terms, based around the interplay of market orientation and market creation within a much wider domain than originally determined. The future for both marketing and art within this relationship should be to perform a more critical role in helping to shape more effective practices that align to the needs of the artist, audience and wider society (Fillis 2011).

Evrard and Colbert (2000) position arts marketing within arts management. They note the legitimacy of arts management at practitioner and academic levels, strengthened by the establishment of the AIMAC international conference in 1991. Arts management involves the promotion of appreciation of the arts, arts managerial knowledge and skills through education. Its remit now reaches beyond arts policy, cultural economics and cultural intervention into other sectors (Colbert 2003). Arts management theory and practice have their roots in business, leisure and aesthetics, which, in turn, have their origins in sociology, economics and social psychology. The role of the consumer and the audience is obviously important when considering arts marketing practice, but customer and market creation are equally valid. The notion of the arts consumer needs to be reinterpreted to include the self as a producer (Cowen and Tabarrok 2000). Determining what is meant by the domain of arts marketing is becoming more difficult as we integrate the arts with culture, leisure, entertainment and a variety of business disciplines (Colbert et al. 2001).

References

Aaker, David A., and George S. Day. 1982. *Consumerism.* New York: Simon and Schuster.

Barksdale, Hiram C., and William R. Darden. 1972. "Consumer attitudes toward marketing and consumerism." *Journal of Marketing* 36, no. 4: pp. 28-35. [doi: 10.2307/1250423]

Baudrillard, Jean. 1988. "Simulacra and Simulations." In *Selected Writings,* edited by Mark Poster. Stanford: Stanford University Press.

Baumol, William J. 1986. "Unnatural value: or art investment as floating crap game." *The American Economic Review* 76, no. 2: pp. 10-14.

Beatty, Sharon E., and M. Elizabeth Ferrell. 1998. "Impulse buying: Modeling its precursors." *Journal of retailing* 74, no. 2: pp. 169-191. [doi: 10.1016/S0022-4359(99)80092-X]

Belk, Russell W., et al. 1991. "Collecting in a Consumer Culture." In *SV - Highways and Buyways: Naturalistic Research from the Consumer Behavior Odyssey,* edited by Russell W. Belk. Provo: Association for Consumer Research.

Bellenger, Danny N. & Pradeep K. Korgaonkar. 1980. "Profiling the recreational shopper." *Journal of retailing* 56, no. 3: pp. 77-92.

Bourriaud, Nicolas. 2002. *Relational aesthetics.* Dijon: Les presses du réel.

Campbell, Rachel. 2008. "Art as a financial investment." *Journal of Alternative Investments* 10, no. 4: 64-81. [doi: 10.3905/jai.2008.705533]

Cham, Karen. 2006. "Aesthetics and interactive art." In *Digital visual culture: Theory and practice,* edited by Anna Bentkowska-Kafel, Trish Cashen, and Hazel Gardiner. Chicago: University of Chicago Press.

Colbert, François, et al. 2001. *Marketing culture and the arts.* Montreal: Morin.

Colbert, François. 2003. "Entrepreneurship and leadership in marketing the arts." *International Journal of Arts Management* 6, no. 1: pp. 30-39. [doi: 10.1108/14715200480001354]

Cosmo, Lepota L. 2019. "Contemporaneity, mythologeme and new object." *Art and Design* 2, no. 4: pp. 158-168. [doi: 10.31058/j.ad.2019.24015]

Courty, Pascal, and Mario Pagliero. 2014. "The pricing of art and the art of pricing: Pricing styles in the concert industry." In *Handbook of the Economics of Art and Culture Volume 2,* edited by Victor A. Ginsburgh and David Throsby. Amsterdam: North Holland.

Cowen, Tyler, and Alexander Tabarrok. 2000. "An economic theory of avant-garde and popular art, or high and low culture." *Southern Economic Journal* 67, no. 2: pp. 232-253. [doi: 10.2307/1061469] d'Astous, Alain, Julie Maltais, and Caroline Roberge. 1990. "Compulsive Buying Tendencies of Adolescent Consumers." In *NA - Advances in Consumer Research Volume 17*, edited by Marvin E. Goldberg, Gerald Gorn, and Richard W. Pollay. Provo: Association for Consumer Research.

Denicola, Robert C. 1983. "Applied art and industrial design: a suggested approach to copyright in useful articles." *Minnessota Law Review* 67, no. 4: p. 707.

Eun Park, Ji, Jun Yu, and Joyce Xin Zhou. 2010. "Consumer innovativeness and shopping styles." *Journal of Consumer Marketing* 27, no. 5: pp. 437-446. [doi: 10.1108/07363761011063330]

Evard, Yves, and François Colbert. 2000. "Arts management: a new discipline entering the millennium?" *International Journal of Arts Management* 2, no. 2: pp. 4-13.

Fillis, Ian R. 2011. "The evolution and development of arts marketing research." *Arts Marketing: An International Journal* 1, no. 1: pp. 11-25. [doi: 10.1108/20442081111129842]

Firat, A. Fuat, Nikhilesh Dholakia, and Alladi Venkatesh. 1995. "Marketing in a postmodern world." *European journal of marketing* 29, no. 1: pp. 40-56. [doi: 10.1108/03090569510075334]

Firat, A. Fuat. 1992. "Postmodernism and the marketing organization." *Journal of Organizational Change Management* 5, no. 1: pp. 79-83. [doi: 10.1108/09534819210011006]

Goetzmann, William N., Luc Renneboog, and Christophe Spaenjers. 2011. "Art and money." *American Economic Review* 101, no. 3: pp. 222-226. [doi: 10.3386/w15502]

Grampp, William D. 1989. *Pricing the priceless: art, artists, and economics.* New York: Basic Books.

Guiry, Michael, Anne W. Mägi, and Richard J. Lutz. 2006. "Defining and measuring recreational shopper identity." *Journal of the Academy of Marketing Science* 34, no. 1: pp. 74-83. [doi: 10.1177/0092070305282042]

Horkheimer, Max, and Theodor W. Adorno. 1972. *Dialectic of Enlightenment: Max Horkheimer and Theodor W. Adorno.* New York: Seabury Press.

Humble, Paula N. 2002. "Anti-art and the concept of art." In *A Companion to Art Theory*, edited by Paul Smith, and Carolyn Wilde. Oxford: Blackwell Publishing.

Janssen, Marco A., and Wander Jager. 2001. "Fashions, habits and changing preferences: Simulation of psychological factors affecting market dynamics." *Journal of economic psychology* 22, no. 6: pp. 745-772. [doi: 10.1016/S0167-4870(01)00063-0]

Joselit, David. 2002. "Yippie Pop: Abbie Hoffman, Andy Warhol, and Sixties Media Politics." *Grey Room*, no. 8: pp. 62-79. [doi: 10.1162/15263810260201607]

Kangun, Norman, et al. 1975. "Consumerism and Marketing Management: How do consumers perceive consumerism... and what are the implications of these perceptions for marketing managers?" *Journal of Marketing* 39, no. 2: pp. 03-10. [doi.org: 10.1177%2F002224297503900203]

Kostelanetz, Richard. 2018. *A dictionary of the avant-gardes.* New York: Psychology Press.

Kosuth, Joseph. 1991. *Art After Philosophy and After Collected Writings, 1966-1990.* Cambridge: The MIT Press.

Kotler, Philip. 1977. "From sales obsession to marketing effectiveness." *Harvard Business Review*: 67-75.

Kunzle, David. 1984. "Pop Art as Consumerist Realism." *Studies in Visual Communication* 10, no. 2: pp. 16-33.

Leung, Godfre. 2007. "After the Neo-Avant-Garde? New-Genre Conceptual Art and the Institution of Critique." *Art Journal* 66, no. 4: pp. 109-111. [doi: 10.2307/20068572]

MacRitchie, Lynn. 1996. "Marina Abramovic: Exchanging Energies." *Performance Research* 1, no. 2: pp. 27-34. [doi: 10.1080/13528165.1996.10871487]

Mayyasi, Alex. "Why Is Art Expensive." Priceonomics. (Accessed: October 06, 2020). https://priceonomics.com/why-is-art-expensive/

Mei, Jianping, and Michael Moses. 2002. "Art as an Investment and the Underperformance of Masterpieces." *American Economic Review* 92, no. 5: pp. 1656-1668. [doi: 10.1257/000282802762024719]

Morgan, Robert C. 1994. *Conceptual art: an American perspective.* Jefferson: McFarland.

Mossetto, Gianfranco. 1993. *Aesthetics and economics.* Dordrecht: Springer.

Moxey, Keith. 2012. "Is Modernity Multiple?" *Revista de História da Arte,* no. 10: pp. 50-57.

Muniz, Albert M., and Thomas C. O'Guinn. 2001. "Brand community." *Journal of consumer research* 27, no. 4: pp. 412-432. [doi: 10.1086/319618]

Ogilvy, James. 1990. "This postmodern business." *Marketing and Research Today* 18, no. 1: pp. 04-20.

Pesando, James E., and Pauline M. Shum. 2008. "The auction market for modern prints: Confirmations, contradictions, and new puzzles." *Economic Inquiry* 46, no. 2: pp. 149-159. [doi: 10.1111/j.1465-7295.2007.00070.x]

Phelan, Peggy. 2004. "Marina Abramović: witnessing shadows." *Theatre Journal* 56, no. 4: pp. 569-577. [doi: 10.1353/tj.2004.0178]

Rancière, Jacques. 2014. "Rethinking Modernity." *Diacritics* 42, no. 3: pp. 06-20. [doi: 10.1353/dia.2014.0017]

Reitlinger, Gerald. 1982. *The economics of taste: the rise and fall of picture prices 1760-1960.* New York: Hacker Art Books.

Reyburn, Scott. "Can an Economist's Theory Apply to Art?" The New York Times. (Accessed: October 06, 2020). nytimes.com/2014/04/21/arts/international/Can-an-Economists-Theory-Apply-to-Art.html

Reynolds, Kristy E., Jaishankar Ganesh, and Michael Luckett. 2002. "Traditional malls vs. factory outlets: comparing shopper typologies and implications for retail strategy." *Journal of Business Research* 55, no. 9: pp. 687-696. [doi: 10.1016/S0148-2963(00)00213-7]

Sagot-Duvauroux, Dominique. 2003. "Art prices." In *A Handbook of Cultural Economics,* edited by Ruth Towse. Northampton: Edward Elgar.

Schroeder, Jonathan E. 2008. "Brand Culture: Trade marks, marketing and consumption." In *Trade marks and brands: An Interdisciplinary Critique,* edited by Jane C. Ginsburg, Lionel Bently, and Jennifer Davis. Cambridge: Cambridge University Press.

Schwarz, Arturo. 1997. *The complete works of Marcel Duchamp* 2. London: Thames and Hudson.

Sharp, Joanne, Venda Pollock, and Ronan Paddison. 2005. "Just art for a just city: Public art and social inclusion in urban regeneration." *Urban Studies* 42, no. 5-6: pp. 1001-1023. [doi: 10.1080/00420980500106963]

Smith, Terry. 2006. "Contemporary art and contemporaneity." *Critical Inquiry* 32, no. 4: pp. 681-707. [doi: 10.1086/508087]

Turley, Lou W., and Ronald E. Milliman. 2000. "Atmospheric effects on shopping behavior: a review of the experimental evidence." *Journal of business research* 49, no. 2: pp. 193-211. [doi: 10.1016/S0148-2963(99)00010-7]

Velthuis, Olav. 2003. "Symbolic meanings of prices: Constructing the value of contemporary art in Amsterdam and New York galleries." *Theory and Society* 32, no. 2: pp. 181-215. [doi: 10.1023/A:1023995520369]

Velthuis, Olav. 2004. "An interpretive approach to meanings of prices." *The Review of Austrian Economics* 17, no. 4: pp. 371-386.

Vermeulen, T. J. V., and R. van den Akker. 2014. "Art criticism and metamodernism." *ArtPulse* 19, no. 3: pp. 22-27.

Wang, Tian-si. 2003. "An Investigation into the Marketing Civilization." *Hebei Academic Journal*, no. 1: w/p.

Ward, Frazer. 1997. "Some relations between conceptual and performance art." *Art Journal* 56, no. 4: pp. 36-40. [doi: 10.2307/777718]

Youn, Seounmi, and Ronald J. Faber. 2000. "Impulse buying: its relation to personality traits and cues." *Advances in Consumer Research* 27, no. 1: pp. 179-185.

Chapter 5

Building Soft Power?

China in the Global Cultural Markets

Gladys Pierpauli & Mariano Turzi

Instituto Superior de Enseñanza Radiofónica (ISER) / Universidad del CEMA, Argentina

Abstract

This chapter analyzes the People's Republic of China as an actor in global cultural markets. The first section reviews the existing conceptualization of culture as a component of international relations in its two dimensions: as a constitutive element of social subjects and as an instrument incorporated in a diplomatic strategy. The first deals with the links at the level of civil society, the second understood as the state's soft power. The second section reveals China as a consumer and producer of cultural goods globally, its magnitude, growth, global economic impacts and the formation of a global cultural canon. The conclusions present public policy implications and avenues for future research.

Keywords: China; cultural relations; globalization; public policies; soft power.

* * *

1. Introduction: Culture and International Relations

Culture is one of the most discussed and disputed concepts in the social sciences. Its polysemy and diversity of methodological approaches make the concept inherently complex and contested. It includes a broad range of meanings from individual attitudes to social relations. Across a wide range of areas or dimensions, culture configures different patterns of human interaction and determines the balance cooperation / conflict, individualism / collectivism, harmony / control, secularism/religiosity (Bond and Lun 2017), certainty / uncertainty and modes of exercising power. (Hofstede 2003) A culture thus defined is made up of a multiplicity of elements that are in competition and controversy. When approaching culture as a collective construction, the multiple factors that shape it are immediately apparent: national, ethnic, religious, organizational, familial, psychological and social. Individuals can use fragments of culturally recognized behaviors to satisfy their own ends. Berger calls cultures plausibility structures, sociocultural contexts within which belief systems and meanings make sense or are plausible. The beliefs and meanings that individuals and groups possess are supported by the interrelation between sociocultural processes and institutions. Establishing a definitive definition of culture is beyond the scope of this work. However, we will establish three main ways to understand its impact on international relations: culture as identity (social dimension), culture as industry (economic dimension) and culture as diplomacy (political dimension).

Culture as Identity

What is commonly referred to as "The arts" or "Fine arts" encompasses[1] the modes of expression that use skill or imagination in the creation of aesthetic objects, environments, or experiences. Music, art, literature, sports and even gastronomy make up an imaginary of a national or regional concrete identity. Culture as identity implies understanding the values, worldviews and factors that structure human relations. It constitutes a formative totalizing corpus of beliefs structuring specific cognitive and motivational factors (at the individual level) and different normative expectations (at the collective level). If cultural variables structure social, political and commercial behaviors, then the definition, communication and negotiation of objectives and interests are also culturally—if not determined—at least strongly conditioned (Jahoda 2012). Understanding the universality or particularity of standards Chinese morals and values in the context of the rise of Beijing to global prominence would thus be of critical importance for the future of world affairs (Iriye 1979; Nau and Ollapally 2012; Gan 2019).

Stuart Hall (1997) has compellingly argued against a homogeneous or unitary concept of culture in the style of Samuel Huntington (1993). The identity dimension of culture thus becomes a marker of political belonging in a world of multiple identities Hall (2002) defines hybridization as a process of *transculturation*, key cultural processes that operate between cultures and peoples forced to interact but that until now have been strongly differentiated. Culture in the singular implies multiple social and cultural forms within the

[1] Traditional categories within the arts include literature (poetry, drama, story), visual arts (painting, drawing, sculpture), graphic arts (painting, drawing, design, and forms on flat surfaces), plastic arts (sculpture, modeling), decorative arts (enamelwork, furniture design, mosaic, etc.), performing arts (theatre, dance, music), music and architecture (including interior design).

same context, a cross-cultural pollination or adaptation. Hybridization (Stockhammer 2011) creates new cultural identities and even cultural subjects. The cultural bond constitutes a symbolic codification of the economic and political experience. Hybridization pushes to transcend cultural stereotypes beyond simplistic or reductionist descriptions. Creates a cross-cultural or intercultural space in constant re-definition and re-signification. The growing transcultural space occupied by China is—we posit—an expression of a new vector of globalization. Theoretically, this raises the question of to what extent it will lead to a reconceptualization of culture (García Canclini 2006) inasmuch it constitutes an international, unstable, open, incoherent space formed through the juxtaposition and co-presence of different intercultural forces, discourses and reciprocal effects.

Culture as Politics

A second way of conceptualizing culture is as an instrument of social construction, a tool of statecraft and public policy. Culture, thus understood, is a reflection that informs about the specific ways in which societies structure power relations in and through institutions, organize groups to achieve goals and promote economic activity. For international relations, this dimension is of fundamental importance for three reasons. The first is decoding Chinese soft power in a context of transition of the world (dis)order (Turzi 2017) and the rise of non-western patterns of organization of global interactions. The question here is whether cultural factors shape differential patterns of international interaction. The second way of approaching culture is as an opportunity to project a national image, evinced in political marketing activities such as "country brands." Governments have often used culture in foreign policy, promoting their own languages, music, media, and views abroad. In this case, the proliferation of Confucius Institutes around the world by China is no different from the promotion of the Dante Alighieri Association for the teaching of Italian, the Alliance Française for French, the British Council or ICANA for English or the Goethe Institut for German. The third is because international trade in cultural goods and services with China itself is largely in the hands of state actors with strong ties -political and financial- to the Chinese Communist Party. Thus, the cultural plane of Sino-Latin American relations is, at the same time, a plane of political and state relations (Wei and Xia 2008; Zang et al. 2012; Fang et al. 2012).

2. Overview of Creative Industries

For the United Nations Educational, Scientific and Cultural Organization (UNESCO 2000), the cultural and creative industries are: "those sectors of organized activity whose main objective is the production or reproduction, promotion, dissemination or commercialization of goods, services and activities with cultural, artistic or heritage content." This means the segment of the economy related to film and television, music, audio and video, the publishing industry, the recording sector, interactive and recreational software, advertising, design and architecture. In 2013, the Inter-American Development Bank (IDB) called the creative and cultural economy the Orange Economy (Buitrago Restrepo and Duque Márquez 2013). It encompasses film, advertising, television, animation, video games, the publishing industry, the music industry, fashion and design. In this paper, we will adopt this definition due to the emphasis that the IDB places on the component of innovation, entrepreneurship and creativity. The notion behind the orange economy is that ideas are transformed into goods and services. Knowledge has an impact - macro and micro- on international competitiveness.

According to the latest United Nations Conference on Trade and Development report (UNCTAD 2019) on the global creative economy, international trade in creative goods has experienced growth: total exports of creative goods increased in the period 2003-2012 by 47% percent to US$474 billion and imports 56%, although to less than US$400 billion. The global growth rates of exports of creative goods have increased by more than 7% in the period 2002-2015. In the same period, the value of the global creative goods market doubled from US$208 billion in 2002 to US$509 billion in 2015. In emerging economies—led by China—the increase was 212%. Asia surpasses all other regions with US$228 billion in creative exports, almost doubling Europe. China; Hong Kong (SAR); India; Singapore; Taiwan, Province of China; Turkey; Thailand; Malaysia; Mexico and the Philippines were the top 10 developing economies that stimulated world trade in creative goods. According to the report, the income generated by the creative and cultural industries in the world exceeded US $ 2.25 billion, 3% of world GDP. Moreover, in terms of employment, the cultural and creative industries employed nearly 30 million people worldwide in 2015, according to UNESCO. Unlike other segments of the economy, the sector contributes more to consolidate cultural identity and social cohesion.

3. China in the Global Culture Markets

According to UNCTAD, China is the world's largest individual exporter and importer of creative goods and services. China's creative goods trade between 2002 and 2015 had an average annual growth rate of 14%. In 2002, China's creative goods trade was US$32 billion. By 2014, this figure had increased more than five times, totaling US$191.4 billion. China has thus become the main force behind the growth of the creative economy in the last decade and a half: in 2015, its exports were four times greater than those of the United States.

China owned 32% of the global creative goods market, compared to 8% in the United States.

The global art market has risen at an annualized rate of 5.3% since 1985 according to Citi (Citibank 2020), achieving similar rates of return to developed investment grade fixed income (6.5%) and high yield fixed income (8.1%), acting as an asset class to diversify investment portfolios. According to the Global Art Market Report (McAndrew 2020), global sales of art and antiques reached an estimated US$64.1 billion in 2019, down 5% year-on-year, returning the market to just above its 2017 level. There were an estimated 310,810 companies operating in the global art and antiques market, employing close to 3 million people. The world art trade also spent US$19.9 billion on a range of ancillary and external support services directly linked to their businesses, supporting 368,860 jobs. The three major art hubs, the US, the UK, and China, continued to account for a majority of the value. The United States is the leader (44% of the market), and the United Kingdom (20%) recovered the second place that it had lost in 2017 to China (which, due to the tensions and uncertainty of the trade war, fell to 18%).[2] The three major art hubs continued to account for 82% of the value of global sales in 2019.

Beginning in 2009, the newly booming Chinese market and a rapid bounce back in sales in the US pushed the international market up to a high of just under US$65 billion by 2011. The sharp ascent in China halted in 2012, leading to a temporary contraction in global sales values. The 2009-2011 boom led China to temporarily become the largest global art market, with sales of US$19.5 billion in 2011. However, a sharp contraction in sales of 30% in 2012 meant this was a temporary position. The slow and declining sales up to 2016 rebounded in 2017, thereafter declining for two consecutive years. The Chinese market in 2019 was 10% lower than its level a decade earlier. Sales fell by 10% in 2019 to reach US$11.7 billion. China's Poly Auction was the third-largest global auction company, with public auction sales of US$1.1 billion. 80% of their sales by value took place in Beijing, with sales in Hong Kong accounting for 14%. And China Guardian regained its fourth position in the global ranks, increasing sales 9% to US$952 million, with 89% in Beijing and 11% in Hong Kong. The art market in China is driven by the liberal business regulatory

[2] President Trump's U.S. tax overhaul eliminated the use of the United States Section 1031 Exchange as it relates to art, whereby art collectors could defer the capital gains on the sale of an artwork by reinvesting the proceeds in a "like kind" artwork within a specific period of time. A trade deal between U.S. and China reached in 2019 will create a 25% tariff on "all artworks that originated in China, regardless of how they entered the United States." The deal includes original paintings, drawings, sculptures, and antiques over 100 years old.

environment in Hong Kong, which has secured it a position as the main gateway to international sales in Asia. And Beijing is critical as a cultural district because of the 58 registered cultural and creative companies in the country; Beijing has 21, with a total market value of more than US$46 billion. The looming debt crisis, trade war and other economic issues dampened demand. And the effects of the COVID-19 pandemic are still unclear (as the effects of online art sales are not clear), leading to a cautious climate for both buyers and sellers.

According to the Motion Picture Association of America (MPAA 2019), global consumer spending on theatrical and home entertainment markets reached US$96.8 billion worldwide. Box office sales in world cinema and theater reached a record US$47.8 billion in 2018, a growth of 17.7% year-on-year. Consumer spending on home entertainment also increased globally in 2018 to exceed US$55 billion. The Chinese movie box office set a record for the Lunar New Year holiday with US$852 million and a billed annual total of US$9 billion in ticket sales. Attendance per capita was highest among Latin American (4.5 times) and Asian (4.3) audiences. In fact, for 2019, consulting firm PwC estimated that total "filmed entertainment" (TV and video) revenue exceeded US$104 billion worldwide, with China accounting for more than 25%.

Emerging markets also fueled overseas revenue of American movies. The Chinese market is increasingly attractive as a destination for film consumption. Co-productions[3] are a way for Chinese films to go global while foreign films gain access to the Chinese market. Collaboration and cross investment between Hollywood and China is another. Between 1997 and 2013, China invested in 11 of the 100 highest-grossing films in the world each year. That number increased to 41 movies for the 2013-2018 period. Currently, half of the countries in the top 10 international box office markets have co-production agreements with China, and the number of co-productions has increased, although they still represent less than 15% of the total. However, they contribute a significant percentage of total box office revenue. Disney has been able to sell its films in China and build a park in Shanghai. In contrast, DreamWorks Animation withdrew from a joint venture with China Media Capital (CMC) to run Oriental DreamWorks. And now ODW is individually owned by CMC.

[3] The Chinese government China Film Co-Production Corporation (中国电影合作制片公司) to foster partnerships with global actors with the aim of generating more Chinese influence. It has an administrative role, manages co-production requests, provides step-by-step guidelines for online applications, and facilitates visas for foreign filming teams and customs clearance for equipment and other materials.

Foreign competition is strictly limited by a quota system: international films in China have a limited quantity that is set at 34 per year. Moreover, indigenous productions receive financial support: cheap land for studios and production companies, subsidies for theaters that show Chinese films. Attendance at screenings of films considered especially patriotic has even been encouraged. As China has gained global preeminence as a box office market, foreign investors and film producers have sought to cooperate with the country. Between 2005 and 2015, the number of private equity funds focused on films in China increased from 5 to 160. Chinese technology companies such as Alibaba Group Holding Ltd. and Tencent invested in the entire production chain, from studios to ticketing companies. For example, as of April 2018, Alibaba owned 48 entertainment companies and was venturing into producing Netflix-style content of its own.) In 2018 alone, Dalian Wanda Group, which bought the iconic American theater chain AMC in 2012, opened the world's largest film studio, which was touted as China's response to Hollywood.

More than a third of China's highest-grossing films in the past two years have been made in the US. But China wants its own films to win the box office, both for financial reasons and for national pride. Industry insiders disclose Chinese investors have been adamant about having "Chinese" scenes in Western movies to make them more sellable in China. The change from "made in China" to "designed in China" also has its counterpart in the film industry: from "made in the world" to "made for China." The plan of the XIII Five-Year Program (2016-2020) for Development and Reform stipulates that the country will help create cultural business groups designed for competition and with high market value. The government plans to make the cultural industry a pillar of the national economy by 2020. Improving infrastructure, strengthening major brands, and promoting consumption are meant to achieve this objective. Government guidelines seek to drive mergers between state cultural companies and mixed property mergers and acquisitions. The report specifies that state cultural companies use the capital market to grow, and it even intends to develop a new internet-based cultural market. The Chinese government lowered barriers to accessing private capital in the creative and cultural sector to drive the development of innovative or specialized private, small and medium-sized cultural enterprises and micro-enterprises. Although the pace of foreign investment has accelerated in China's cultural industry, statistical analysis over ten years have estimated that the effects of foreign direct investment in promoting added value of Chinese cultural industries has not been significant (Wang and Wu 2015).

In the same line, the Central Committee of the Chinese Party (CCP) at the 13th National People's Congress of China in March 2018 unveiled a plan to merge state-owned radio and television stations on a broadcast platform to be called

Zhongguo Zhisheng (中国之声 - Voice of China). China Central Television (CCTV), China International Radio (CRI) and China National Radio (CNR) form the new state media conglomerate, tasked with "better telling the country's stories to the world." The government had already sought to use state media as a means to increase its soft power around the world in late 2016, when China re-launched its global television network, formerly known as China Central Television (CCTV), as a group of six international language channels under a new global media brand, the China Global Television Network (CGTN). The new Chinese media platform will be under the state's Advertising Department and is tasked with improving China's international broadcast capabilities and promoting the convergence of the three platforms. Institutionally, the State Administration of Press, Publications, Cinema, Radio and Television (SAPPFRT-国家新闻出版广电总局) was dissolved, and the State Administration of Radio and Television (NRTA - 国家广电总局) was established. In this way, the press, publication and cinema became centralized under the direct administration of the Advertising Department. The Chinese government has domestic imperatives to attend to newspapers and magazines with long-term financial and operational difficulties; they will be merged, reabsorbed, reorganized or closed. It is estimated that there are 20,000 film and television companies in China that are not economically viable, which could be leading to a bubble in the cultural sector. The fear is a vicious circle like it has already happened with electric cars or solar panels: a) bureaucrats deciding that a favored industry should be generated and be globally competitive, b) directing public funds, c) rushing foreign direct investment, d) market problems and e) collapse. This consolidation in China is vital to understand the current dynamic of its media market.

In addition to the quantitative extension is the qualitative depth. Hollywood is increasingly aware of the Chinese market in its productions. Film studios rely on Chinese theaters to engross bottom lines or turn fiascos into modest hits. The 2018 reboot "Tomb Raider" netted a disappointing $58 million in U.S. theaters, but generated $78 million in China alone. American movies routinely accept alterations to appease Chinese censors. And politically savvy stars stay silent on the country's human rights abuses to avoid being blacklisted. Chinese officials also pressure American studios. This kind of power (Bachrach and Baratz 1963) is as important as invisible: self-censorship and non-decisions about stories that aren't told and Chinese villains that never make it to the big screen. The 2012 "Red Dawn" remake, for example, found MGM swapping out the script's original enemy, China, for North Korean troops at the last minute. Paramount movie adaptation of Max Brooks' "World War Z" novel changed the source material so the zombie outbreak didn't begin in China. The escalation of tensions in 2019 led the industry to the point of no return. And the 2020 spat between Washington and Beijing about the origin of COVID-19 (if it was released by the US government or from a Wuhan lab) means cooperation is poised to end with Hollywood. As an indicator of things to come, Arkansas Sen. Tom Cotton tweeted on April 20, 2020: “Did you know Hollywood is in China's pocket? China funds US movies & studios are desperate for access to the Chinese market. That's why China is never the bad guy in movies. That's why they took Taiwan's flag off Maverick's jacket in Top Gun 2. Time for this to end.”

If the cultural vector in international relations constitutes a space of hybrid representations where local elements are intertwined with external forces, then the position of China in global cultural markets is not strictly economic. The actors and products of culture are representations that aim to reproduce the international reality through non-fiction -written press, international television programs and specialized media- or fiction -literature, cinema, theater or other expressions that appeal to entertainment. (Neumann and Nexon 2006) Besides the analysis of international economic interests and domestic political institutions, a new chapter of critical importance opens up for analysis: China's cultural and creative industries in the Belt and Road Initiative (NDRC 2015). The Action Plan for the Cultural Development of the Belt and Road (2016-20) seeks to support local authorities and the public throughout the countries within the Initiative to explore the historical and cultural heritage along the old Silk Road, making joint investments and promoting cultural exchange with the 67 member countries of the initiative. For this, initiatives such as the Silk Road International Culture Exhibition, the Silk Road International Film Festival and the Silk Road International Book Fair have been established. In the cultural field alone, as of May 2018, there were more than 40 projects covering many fields of the creative cultural industry such as animation (Guangdong Alpha Animation), figure skating and acrobatic ice (Heilongjiang Acrobatic Company), Chinese tea culture (Anhui Keemun Development of Black Tea) or carving, engraving and wood painting (Hebei Bainianqiaojiang Cultural Communication) or traditional silk culture (Silk Wujiang Dingsheng).

4. Conclusions

This chapter distinguished the social and political dimensions of culture (culture as an attribute vs. culture as public policy). In the case of China, economic globalization has allowed China to insert itself into yet another production and consumption sector. Our focus was not on the globalization of Chinese culture, but on the drivers behind Chinese presence in the global culture markets. Rather than focusing on Chinese culture in the world or on Chinese culture as a result of state policy, we adopted an international political economy framework to analyze China in the international cultural markets.

Through this perspective, we could unearth the ideas, interests and institutions structuring Chinese domestic and international (inter)actions in the art, cinema, radio and TV markets.

As an exploratory work, several general lines for future research and public policy emerged. They are beyond the scope of this chapter, but nonetheless important to state and explore.

a) **The conceptualization of the culture variable in current international relations.** It is necessary to incorporate the cultural dimension into the strategies of international economic insertion for different actors and sectors, exploring their methodological and practical interrelations. Discriminating between culture as a variable (individual or social dimension), culture as a market/industry (economic dimension) and culture as an instrument of power (political dimension) allows for a more grounded and solid framework.

b) **Is there a relationship between the governance model and industrial structure or organization?** Is there variation between national cultural characteristics and cultural market operation? Creative and cultural industries or cultural property markets are no exception to political institutions: national laws on intellectual property, regulatory frameworks, legal certainty, tax incentives, access to capital, infrastructure, level of competition and consumer protection will shape the behavior of these sectors.

c) **Is the protection of national culture and identity itself a "national interest"?** Today the global structure of culture is transnational and industrialized and at the same time of growing nationalism, nativism, protectionism and xenophobia. This poses new challenges for governments and economic actors in the field of creative and cultural industries. The export and import of a cultural product have both an economic and a national identity component; wealth and power, interest and influence. Like no other item or sector of the economy, cultural assets reflect values. And those values—deliberately or involuntarily—have the capacity to defend or undermine the current social order, the prevailing economic structures or the dominant political order.

References

Bachrach, Peter, and Morton S. Baratz. 1963 "Decisions and nondecisions: An analytical framework." *American political science review* 57, no. 3: pp. 632-642. [doi: 10.2307/1952568]

Bond, Michael H, and Vivian Miu-Chi Lun. 2017. "Examining religion and well-being across cultures: the cognitive science of religion as sextant." In *Religious Cognition in China,* edited by Ryan G. Hornbeck, Justin L. Barrett, and Madeleine Kang. Cham: Springer.

Buitrago Restrepo, Felipe, and Iván Duque Márquez. 2013. *The orange economy: An infinite opportunity.* Washington DC: Inter-American Development Bank.

Citibank. "The Global Art Market: Drivers of Evolution." Citibank. (Accessed October 6, 2020). privatebank.citibank.com/home/fresh-insight/the-global-art-market-drivers-of-evolution.html

Fang, Ying, Huai-liang Li, and Li-yan Sun. 2012. "Trade Structure and International Competitiveness of Cultural Trade in China." *Commercial Research* 1: w/p.

Gan, Chunsong. 2019. *A Concise Reader of Chinese Culture.* Singapore: Springer.

García Canclini, Néstor. 2006. "La globalización: ¿productora de culturas híbridas?" In *Construyendo colectivamente la convivencia en la diversidad: los retos de la inmigración,* edited by Manuel Encina, and Javier Montañés. Sevilla: Atrapasueños.

Hall, Stuart, Lynne Seagal, and Peter Osborne. 1997. "Stuart Hall: Culture and power." *Radical Philosophy* 86: pp. 24-41.

Hall, Stuart. 2002. "Political belonging in a world of multiple identities." In *Conceiving cosmopolitanism: Theory, context, and practice,* edited by Steven Vertovec and Robin Cohen. Oxford: Oxford University Press.

Hofstede, Geert. 2003. *Culture's consequences: Comparing values, behaviors, institutions and organizations across nations.* Thousand Oaks: Sage publications.

Huntington, Samuel P. 1993. "The clash of civilizations." *Foreign affairs* 72, no. 3: pp. 22-49.

Iriye, Akira. 1979. "Culture and power: international relations as intercultural relations." *Diplomatic History* 3, no. 2: pp. 115-128. [doi: 10.1111/j.1467-7709.1979.tb00305.x]

Jahoda, Gustav. 2012. "Critical reflections on some recent definitions of "culture"." *Culture & Psychology* 18, no. 3: pp. 289-303. [doi: 10.1177/1354067X12446229]

McAndrew, Claire. 2020. *The Art Market 2020.* Basel: Art Basel and UBS.

MPAA. "THEME (theatrical and home entertainment market environment) Report 2019." Motionpictures. (Accessed: October 06, 2020). motionpictures.org/wp-content/uploads/2019/03/MPAA-THEME-Report-2018.pdf

Nau, Henry R., and Deepa M. Ollapally, eds. 2012. *Worldviews of aspiring powers: domestic foreign policy debates in China, India, Iran, Japan and Russia.* Oxford: Oxford University Press.

NDRC. "Action plan on the Belt and Road Initiative." Chinese Government. (Accessed: October 06, 2015). english.www.gov.cn/archive/publications/2015/03/30/content_281475080249035.htm

Neumann, Iver B., and Daniel H. Nexon. 2006. "Introduction: Harry Potter and the study of world politics." In *Harry Potter and international relations,* edited by Iver B. Neumann, and Daniel H. Nexon, Lanham: Rowman & Littlefield.

Stockhammer, Philipp W., ed. 2011. *Conceptualizing cultural hybridization: a transdisciplinary approach.* New York: Springer.

Turzi, Mariano L. 2007. *Todo lo que necesitás saber sobre el (des) orden mundial.* Buenos Aires: Paidós Argentina.

UNCTAD. 2019. "Creative economy outlook: Trends in international trade in creative industries 2002–2015. Country Profiles: 2005–2014." In *United Nations Conference on Trade and Development*, edited by UNCTAD. Geneva: UNCTAD.

UNESCO. 2000. *World Culture Report*. UNESCO Publishing.

Wang, Jianping, and Haibing Wu. 2015. "Empirical Research on the Influence of FDI on China's Cultural Industry: Analysis Based on VAR Model." In *Proceedings of 2014 1st International Conference on Industrial Economics and Industrial Security*, edited by Meng Gang Li, et al. Berlin: Springer.

Wei, Ting, and Bao-lian Xia. 2008. "Analysis of the Current situation and Reasons of China's Movie & TV Cultural Trade." *International Economics and Trade Research* 24, no. 3: p. 65.

Zang, Xin, Zhu Lin, and Jun Shao. 2012. "Cultural proximity, economic development and export of cultural products." *Finance & Trade Economics*, no. 10: pp. 102-110. [doi: 10.2991/icesem-18.2018.44]

Chapter 6

Culture of Resistance

The Effect of the 1943 Bengal famine on Bengali Theater, Literature, and Painting

Aritra De

Texas Tech University, USA

Abstract

The Bengal famine of 1943 was one of the most devastating and controversial chapters of the history of India that took the lives of almost 3 million Bengalis. My attempt in this chapter is not to analyze technicalities of divergent aspects of art and culture of Bengal that had been impacted as a result of the famine, but as a student of history, I would holistically analyze how the event resulted in a paradigm shift by which Bengali art shifted from romanticizing nature and mythological content to a form of protest and socio-political awareness. I will specifically focus on Bengali theater, literature, and painting to analyze the abovementioned change and will use Bengali newspapers and works of the then artists, among others, to comprehend how this particular event significantly inspired them to turn their attention to realism. In doing so, I will briefly discuss the nature of the famine for the non-specialized readers and underscore how poor harvest of 1942 exacerbated the famine as a result of the British policy of restricting the supply of food from other parts of India to hoard food grain for the British soldiers who were residing in Bengal. British snollygosters tried to make profit out of the situation by participating in the black-marketing of rice.

Consequently, growing nationalist sentiments intensified because of the economic havoc, and Bengali artists responded to this situation accordingly. The Communist Party of India started conducting street theater and decided to highlight the hard realities of the famine not only to attract people's attention but also to raise funds through their performances. Bengali Literature, similarly, witnessed a change because of the event as the authors instead of highlighting romantic entanglement of a stable society decided to use their work as a means to mobilize people not only to express their solidarity towards their fellow citizens but also to rise up against the British rule. Many Bengali painters used their painting for the abovementioned purpose. Therefore, in this chapter, I will discuss the ways in which the economic repercussions of this man-made devastation were portrayed through different Bengali art-forms as artists began to redefine their respective approach to realism so that they could channel the popular sentiment against the colonial government and could harness a nationalist sentiment among the Bengalis in particular, and Indians in general.

Keywords: Bengal famine; cultural production; economic repercussions; Indian art; social protest.

* * *

The 1940s was a tumultuous period for the world as the Second World War ravaged Europe and Asia, and while the warfront saw the deaths of millions, colonial India witnessed a disastrous famine that destroyed Bengal and parts of Bihar, taking the lives of millions who died from starvation and disease. While much has been known about the general causes and consequences of the 1943 famine in Bengal, it is largely unknown to the world as it coincided with the rising tide of anti-fascist and anti-imperial resistance throughout colonial India. During the critical years of the Second World War, the province of Bengal became an important strategic asset for the British and the Allied forces as one of the major centers of food resources that were being collected for the war front. In Bengal, rice was harvested three times, as in *boro*, *aus*, and *aman* (three different types of rice) based on the seasonal variations in Bengal, but by late 1942, the production of rice showed a relative shortage due to fluctuations in weather that was further aggravated by a cyclone and flood that destroyed crops and paddy fields. Moreover, the situation deteriorated as the British decided to favor the comfort of their soldiers and citizens over the suffering of the Bengali people through hoarding and stock-piling of food grains as well as refusing to send in alternate food grains such as wheat as a relief to the famine-affected regions of Bengal. It is important to note here that the effects of the famine were borne mostly by the rural population compared to the cities as the latter consisted of elite Indians and British who benefited from the British rationing systems that favored the rich and wealthy. In all, the fatality of the famine and its consequent effects has been estimated at around two million lives and more from various diseases.

In this essay, I argue that the famine of 1943 was a significant event that witnessed the rise of a cultural resistance across Bengal through its rich art and literary heritage. This was reinforced by the plight and suffering of a large section of the population and the dismantling of the rural-urban and class-caste divide brought about by the famine. In this context, I intend to show how Bengali theater, literature, and painting witnessed a paradigm shift when a significant number of artists expressed their interest in social realism. At the same time, it is important to understand that the content of social realism transcended political affiliations, and through this essay, I will demonstrate how artists and writers created works that were devoted simply to the cause. In doing so, I will briefly provide a background to the emergence of cultural resistance across Bengal since the 1920s. Following this, I will discuss the importance of the play "Nabanna" during the years of the famine and how it reinforced the cultural movement that had begun to shift from romanticism to social and political awareness. I will then present some of the significant literary contributions by renowned authors like Bibhutibhusan Bandyopadhyay, Manik Bandyopadhyay, and Tarasankar Bandyopadhyay, who undertook the despondency and suffering of the Bengali people during the famine as the content of their work in an attempt to raise social consciousness. In the final section of this essay, I will discuss the impact of art and painting as one of the principal tools of cultural resistance, not only against the exploitative nature of colonial rule but as a means to mobilize people to support famine relief campaigns.

Bengal had a rich history of political awareness and resistance to colonial rule, and the shift towards realism within this cultural resistance can be traced back to the 1920s and 1930s when contemporary artists took up socio-political and economic exploitation as themes for their creation. One of the prime examples of the shift in focus of contemporary Bengali writers from the romanticism of nature to the ugly and harsh realities of life, and the complexity of relations between people, was the Kallol Group. Writers of this group devoted their attention to the downtrodden and the disenfranchised people of Bengal who were doubly oppressed by the zamindars and landlords under the cruel colonial administrative laws. This trend continued when the Progressive Writer's Association and Indian People's Theater Association was founded to expose the social reality of the contemporary Indian people. The Progressive Writer's Association was founded in 1936 when many prominent artists from all over India gathered together in the city of Lucknow to condemn the rise of fascism in Europe and to safeguard freedom of cultural expression, and it became a platform to express international solidarity along with depicting indigenous misery. For instance, "a meeting was held on 26 July 1935, in Calcutta to protest against the Italian invasion of Abyssinia, and an "Anti-war Day" was observed on 1 August 1935." (Mitra 1979/1980, 116) Similarly, the association in their manifesto made it clear that the Indian writers should not merely become an observer of the contemporary social, political, and economic exploitation; rather, "the new literature of India must deal with the basic problems of our existence today-the problem of hunger and poverty, social backwardness and political subjugation" (Panikkar 2011, 16).

Correspondingly, in the arena of painting, a transition of artistic style and the subject was taking place since the 1920s in the aftermath of the Russian Revolution, when along with the European models of abstract expressionist arts, the Russian model of portraying naturalistic and simplistic human form and life encouraged Indian artists with a need to analyze both. The influence of the Russian model led the Communist Party of India to initiate a cultural movement where it commissioned artists and painters to portray the suffering and frustration of the common people. The CPI dominated all spheres of the cultural movement during the 1940s, especially those around the Bengal Famine of 1943, and this was possible due to the removal of the ban on the party by the colonial government. The anti-colonial stance of the party during this time shifted in support of Allied war efforts against Nazi Germany, especially after Hitler attacked the Soviet Union. Consequently, while political activities of the party were still under scrutiny, the CPI used alternative means to continue their resistance and create awareness against the colonial exploitations, which found vivid expression through drama, theatre, art, and literature.

The progressive cultural movement, therefore, broadened its scope to the realm of theater and subsequently, in 1943, the Indian People's Theater Association was established to express people's discontent through theater. "After the August 1942 resolution of "Quit India," when the national leaders were put behind bars, and the people were groveling in the slush of despair, the Communist Party shouldered the responsibility of organizing masses against Japanese fascism and relief for and rehabilitation of the famine-stricken people. The IPTA tried to arouse the conscience of the community and to make the people work for this great humanist endeavor." (Mitra 1979/1980, 118) The IPTA, being one of the oldest theatre associations in India, grew into a strong political instrument of protest against colonial rule and a medium of public awareness and resistance against fascism. While many famous Bengali dramatists and actors led the movement of mass resistance through their works, one significant play that was put forward by IPTA in 1944 deserves mention in this essay. "Nabanna," written by Bijon Bhattacharya and co-directed by Shambhu Mitra, was extremely powerful in drawing the attention of middle-class and upper-class Bengalis who were greatly detached from the disastrous nature of the famine of 1943.

Moreover, the rural-urban divide that became increasingly wide as the famine ravaged the countryside while the cities prevailed through colonial subsidization schemes led artists such as Bhattacharya to take up their theatrical performances as a means to instigate empathy among the people in the city and to call for united resistance. "Nabanna" was presented through several episodes that were dramatically different from one another, and yet the audience would be able to comprehend the complexity and interconnectedness of the events it portrayed. Inspired by real events of the Quit India movement that was surging through the country during 1942 and the succeeding famine and war, the play begins with glimpses of Aminpur village and the turmoil of the villagers in the hands of local agents of the British government. The initial acts are presented in a fast pace fashion revealing the devastation of the countryside and the loss of lives following a cyclone, and it is here where the central character, Pradhan Samaddar, a landed cultivator, is introduced who lost his sons to unknown reasons and also a considerable part of his land to the natural disaster. Therefore, through these scenes, Bhattacharya wanted to display the harsh realities of the time where social barriers and distinctions broke down as a landed cultivator like Samaddar became a beggar similar to his poor landless neighbor Dayal. The following scenes show the migration of villagers to the cities in search of alternate livelihood as their homes are destroyed, but there is a similar image of oppression and violence, death, and destruction in the city. The scenes demonstrated the desperation of the Samaddar family as they roamed the streets in search of food that stood in stark contrast to the demonstrations of illegal wealth and display of excess food within certain households in the city, celebrating weddings in the atmosphere of death and desolation.

The act ends with the return of some prosperity to the countryside as well as the Samaddar family as the villagers who had once been forced to abandon their homes return and collectively farm to improve their livelihood. The inherent message of the play becomes clear where Bhattacharya revealed that just as the people fought against the tides of famine and natural disasters, similarly, resistance to and success over colonial oppression and fascism was possible through the determination and unity of the Indian people. "Nabanna," therefore, was a conscious effort on the part of Bhattacharya to highlight the intrinsic layers of people's resistance where, while the play visually demonstrated the struggle and horror of the famine of 1943, it had the larger concept of Indian independence at heart that he built through the different episodes culminating in the victory of people's resistance in the last act.

Bengal's rich artistic and literary culture was not limited to theatre and dramatic representations, but it percolated into every sphere of life, which was best exemplified through novels and short stories. In this section, I discuss some of the works of famous Bengali writers who, through their work, have highlighted the effects of the 1943 famine, especially in the countryside. These works, irrespective of their creators' ideological motivations, collectively allowed thousands of Bengalis to acknowledge the plight of the poor and the impoverished. Scholars argue that the effect of the Bengal famine of 1943 was more disastrous for the rural Bengal in general and landless peasants in particular because of the distinct socio-economic structure of the countryside. One such theory was put forward by economist Amartya Sen, who, through his "Entitlement Theory," explained why the famine was so devastating for certain sections of the people, especially those in the countryside. By "Entitlement," Sen means the manner of acquiring food either through self-cultivation, purchase, employment, or through barter and donation of food items. (Devereux 2001, 246) Therefore, for Sen in the desperate times of famines, the amount of food is not as important as the means of acquiring it, which was lost to a large section of the population during the devastating years of the 1940s. As Sen indicates, for farmers who owned lands, the entitlement over food grains allowed them to cultivate and consume their harvest to an extent. However, for fishermen, workers, and agricultural laborers—who constituted the largest percentage of the rural population killed in the famine—the hoarding of grains and the resultant rise in food prices was disastrous. It is important to note that the people of rural Bengal's monetary condition was in no way significantly better before the famine of 1943, but rather a rural barter system and sufficient agricultural produce enabled them to feed themselves. During the years of the famine, nevertheless, the British war effort resulted in the stockpiling of food grains, creating an artificial food shortage which not only increased the price of food grains but disproportionately altered the value of rice in a barter system, leading to a depreciation of entitlements.

Sen's theory is reflected in many of the works of contemporary writers, one of whom was Bibhutibhusan Bandyopadhyay. Bibhutibhusan was "an admirer of nature and life and consciously avoided the fast city life to embrace the splendor of nature. He felt the beat of the universe and wanted to mingle with this splendid world. To him, the joy of one's life is to spread out one's self to the surrounding universe." (Mukherjee 1975, 35) Although his works depicted the people of the Bengali countryside's misery, their love of rural Bengal and their conscious abandonment of urban lifestyle were often highlighted through his works. Here, I examine two of his famous works, "Ashani Sanket" and "Chaul," where his approach towards the Bengal famine of 1943 was perhaps most directly presented.

His novel "Ashani Sanket" discusses the causative reasons for this unequal food distribution and the inability to procure food despite its availability among the Bengalis during the years of the Second World War and the Bengal famine of 1943. In the novel, the author delves into the Bengali countryside through the lives of an upper-caste Brahmin Gangacharan and his family. Gangacharan was a priest in his village and well-respected in the community, and in return for the religious service, he received rice, other food, and household items that were sufficient for his family. Bibhutibhusan stressed the fact that the exchange of harvest and/or services in rural Bengal was the common way of life, as the value of the goods was mostly measured against the value of other goods rather than monetary transactions. While reflecting the abundance of harvest and availability of food items before 1943, the narrative also reflected the affectionate nature of rural Bengali communities. The stability of the village was shown to be altered drastically in the years leading up to the famine when the price of food grains started to increase, thereby causing panic among the villagers. The author mentioned that while rumors about the rise in food prices and inflation made the rounds at the beginning of 1943, the rural countryside largely neglected such warnings as they believed in the abundance of their lands and that they would never be left hungry. Bibhutibhusan highlighted the innocence and political ignorance of the rural countryside regarding the ongoing Second World War and the consequent colonial policies that were implemented to stock food supplies for the army. However, the villagers' curiosity to comprehend the socio-political and economic situation of Bengal led them to discuss their situation and the war, but the political illiteracy of the people was best exemplified by the author through the following conversations in a soiree of villagers. Some of them remarked that the Japanese army had captured a certain "pur," to which Gangacharan being a savant, responded that the Japanese had managed to capture Singapore.

Before proceeding further, it is important to understand the ramification of the famine on the Bengali caste and class structure, since the economic lives of the Bengalis were very much connected with their class and caste identity. Especially in rural Bengal, the caste hierarchy was strictly enforced and respected over economic status. For instance, a lower-class Brahmin was highly respected and held prominence over a rich low caste landowner. Moreover, Brahmin priests were revered within the community, and hence they were bestowed with goods and grains as a symbol of respect in the society. However, with the 1943 crisis, the increase in food shortages due to inflation and black marketing of grains as well as looting and hoarding by the British disrupted the economic stability of Bengal, as well as the livelihood of millions of Bengalis both in the villages as well as in the cities. As the story proceeds, this economic disruption had a direct impact on the social structure of Bengal as it destabilized the caste hierarchy where a respected upper-caste Brahmin like Gangacharan was falsely accused of stealing rice and who later was shown to beg for the rice to a lower caste landowner to keep his family from starvation and death.

Furthermore, Bibhutibhusan's brilliance in capturing the devastation and horror of the 1943 famine is evident in his short story, "Chaul" (Rice). In the five-page story, the author situated himself as the narrator who encountered a poor middle-aged man with a small child on one of his evenings walks along in the forests of the Manbhum district of Purulia in present-day West Bengal. The author began the story by describing the ambiance of the forest where his bungalow was located and the beautiful greenery and unique wildflowers, which were in stark contrast to the frail, malnourished, and barely clothed bodies of the two humans he encountered. Through their acquaintance, the author learned that the man was a widower with a two-year-old girl. In the absence of any caretaker for his child, he was forced to give up his work as a woodcutter and search for alternative means to earn a living in the big city of Purulia. After failed attempts to find work, he was forced to beg on the streets and find shelter on the porch of a village acquaintance, which was only temporary for the family, as the famine forced them out of their shelter and rendered them homeless once again. Through the story of the widower's life and his struggle to find food for himself and his daughter, the author highlighted the existing condition of a considerable section of the Bengali population even before the famine hit.

Furthermore, as the story proceeds, the narrative shifts from the perspective of the widower to the author himself, where he witnessed the horror of the famine and its effect on the poor and destitute. The descriptions and the feeling of despair among the people are vivid as they grasp the reader with the shock of such images. Through the narrative of his travels, it became evident that the famine was not only ravaging the heartlands of Bengal but also the hinterlands and the regions that are now known as Bihar. The author mentioned how he came across a group of children and some dogs waiting together all day and night in the hopes of acquiring the leftover rice water to feed themselves in a local village school in Bihar. Towards the end of the story, the author arrived at a mining region in Bengal, where thousands of people worked in return for some rice to survive in this devastating time, and in a tragic coincidence, he meets the widower from the forest who was forced to find work in the mines to survive and was on the verge of death from a mining accident. The author ends the story with a heavy heart as he mentioned the hopelessness and pain in the widower's eyes and the stillness of his daughter's eyes while he was being taken to the hospital. The despair of the event shook the author with the question of the daughter's fate now that he was on the cusp of death, leaving her alone in a world that was fighting for two grains of rice and surrounded by skeletal remains of those lost.

Another veteran Bengali writer of that era and a member of the undivided Communist Party of India was Manik Bandyopadhyay, who was closely associated with the Progressive Writer's Association of Bengal. His experience with poverty, along with his great observation skills, enabled him to present the experience of the downtrodden people of Bengal brilliantly. Realizing the inability of the Kallol Group to mirror the subaltern experience, Manik Bandyopadhyay remarked, "they approached the slum-dwellers life from a middle-class point of view. What these writers practiced as realism was a rather superficial thing; it was essence bourgeois sentimentalism expressed differently" (Bhattacharjee 2008, 9). Manik's adherence to Marxist ideals led him to portray the harsh reality of the lives of the rural population, and the people's lived struggles rather than romanticizing the rural countryside and its natural beauty. Here, I examine two of his important works, "Chintamoni" and "Dushashaniya," that addressed the famine of Bengal.

"Chintamoni" highlights the deadly effect the famine had on the villagers of Madhubani, who had a hard time believing that a war in a foreign country could do any harm to the villagers of Bengal. He showed how an already broken and exploitative economic system of rural Bengal, which was dominated by money lenders and exploitative zamindars, collapsed as a result of the famine-like a house of cards. The rise in the price of food grains, scarcity of essential commodities like medicine, clothes, and others is the overarching theme of the story. The author showed how the shortage of clothes became so severe that a thread of cotton became equivalent to the price of gold, and hence the weavers of the village completely lost their jobs since they could not afford to pay for the cotton thread. Similarly, iron was an important commodity during the time of war, and hence the colonial authority made an effort to collect as much iron as possible. The story mentioned how the iron plow, nails, hammer, and other essential commodities were completely wiped out from the village. An ironsmith of the village had to sell his stock of iron to a broker at five rupees while the broker managed to sell it off at 15 rupees.

Manik Bandyopadhyay's "Dushashaniya" similarly portrayed the shortage of clothes in the rural countryside where he showed how the women of the village had no alternative but to go out at night to wash their clothes and take a bath in the pond. In some households, women had to take turns to go out since, in many cases, a household could afford only a single piece of cloth to cover her body. The author also underscored how some women had to cover their bodies with a floormat and also depicted the helplessness of the male members of the family because of their inability to provide their wives with clothes and food. Here, the author blended the Indian mythological epic the "Mahabharata" with the social reality of the present time, when he compared the exploitative nature of the black marketers with the evil prince Dushsyasana, who had committed the act of Draupadi's *vastra-haran* (forcible removal of the clothes) in the story. Bandyopadhyay, in drawing this parallel, signified the lack of clothes for Bengali women as the metaphorical act of *vastra-haran* by the oppressive agents of the colonial state that left the Bengali men powerless similar to that of Draupadi's five husbands in the epic.

Another stalwart in the literary field, Tarasankar Bandyopadhyay, rose to prominence when the authors like Manik and Bibhutibhusan had already established themselves with their respective literary style. Unlike Manik Bandyopadhyay's communist inclination and Bibhuti Bhusan's apparent non-political standpoint, Tarasankar's ideological reasoning resembled Gandhian philosophical ideals, but his personal experience of rural Bengal and his ability to analyze and portray sociological justification of human action managed to enrich his readers with the varied experience of both colonial and indigenous exploitation. His writings show how the Second World War disrupted the supply of food and kerosene, particularly after the fall of Java and Burma to the Japanese hand. Food shortage, which was accompanied by black marketing of essential commodities, gradually pushed the city of Calcutta towards dark uncertainty where on the one hand, thousands of people struggled to survive with or without proper nutrition, a section of the wealthy population, on the other hand, managed to acquire fortune out of this unprecedented situation. In this section, I analyze two of his famous works, "Mannantar" and "Bobakanna," where he highlighted the effects of the Bengal famine on the colonial city of Calcutta and in the rural countryside, respectively.

Tarasankar Bandyopadhyay's novel "Mannantar" mirrors the condition of colonial Calcutta during the turbulent years of the 1943 famine where the protagonist of the story Kanai, tries his best to support his family but fails to meet their demands because of their extreme greed. The story proceeds with some unexpected turn to uncover the devastating effects of famine. The novel shows how Kanai's neighbor got heckled by a moneylender as the former failed to return the debt with interest, which was a very common phenomenon during the time of the famine. People, desperate for food, often had to borrow money to support their families and, in extreme circumstances, had to sell their family members. Tara Sankar's novel portrayed the same situation when Kanai found Geeta, the daughter of the man who got heckled by the moneylender, crying on the street as her parents made a deal with a pimp to push her into the abyss of prostitution so that their family could be saved. Kanai also provides private tuition to a son of a wealthy family whose prosperity increased because of the famine due to the black-marketing of rice and other essential commodities. The author unveils how Kanai's student proudly remarks that if their storage stopped supplying rice for a week, the entire Bengal would starve for eight days. The novel also shows how the war and the consequent famine forced the youth of Calcutta to participate in unlawful activities and take up unconventional methods of earning to support their family. The author mentions Geeta's brother, who got involved in black-marketing film tickets and used to buy sugar at a government-regulated price from designated government stores and sold it at a much higher price. Thousands of young people, both from Calcutta and from the rural hinterlands, irrespective of their caste, took the profession of polishing shoes for the European soldiers in the streets of Calcutta to sustain their family while some others begged on the street for food.

In contrast to the effects of the famine on the city of Calcutta, Tarasankar's "Bobakanna" depicted the socio-economic situation of the Bengal famine in the rural countryside and the suburbs of Calcutta. He shows how the catastrophic effect of famine dismantled the strong traditional belief-systems of the Bengali society, where the horror of famine led a priest of a village to abandon his religious activity while a doctor from the same village lost his faith in science. Like in "Mannantar," the author highlighted the unlawful activities that gave a section of the Bengali people the opportunity to make a profit out of people's helplessness. Seasonal flooding in Bengal was a common phenomenon, but the war and the resultant food shortage significantly exacerbated the situation. After the flood, various diseases like cholera and malaria broke out in the Bengali hinterlands, and as a result, a section of Bengalis started to take advantage of the situation by black-marketing medicine along with stockpiling grains. The author mentions how the Quinine injection, which is used to treat malaria, became unavailable during the period and, to cover up this shortage of the actual drug, black marketeers would sell false medicines by diluting wheat in spirit. Through his stories, Tarasankar emphasized the need to survive among the Bengali people in these dark times by any means possible, which was a distinctive trait in his literary style.

The purpose of these writers, irrespective of their political affiliation, was not to conform with the denial of a section of the population about the social turmoil of the period, but rather to underscore and document the mass suffering of Bengal as a means to awaken them. Their artistic representation, hence, in no way intended to comfort people's minds but to de-alienate them to social reality. Despite this similarity, there are a few particular characteristics that distinguished the style of their works. Although presenting the reality of the Bengal famine, Bibhutibhusan's work and his immense love for nature were not intended to generate extreme anger among the people. He was a transcendentalist in his mentality and quoted the American transcendentalist Ralph Waldo Emerson to express his literary style: "every literary man should embrace solitude as a bride" (Mukherjee 1975, 35). As a result, despite witnessing the wrath of famine, his characters managed to find solace in the village and tried to survive the situation by retaining domestic stability. Manik Bandyopadhyay's work, on the other hand, is devoid of any romanticism where the presence of social realism is as strong as his ideological commitment. His works necessitated his readers not only to witness the suffering of the people of Bengal, which was caused by the famine but also to motivate them against the divergent forms of oppression. His works are a direct representation of social reality whose candor and conscious absence of encomium of nature is intended to shake people by loudly mirroring the image of hungry Bengal so that they, irrespective of their caste, class and religious background, could come forward to ward off colonial exploitation and mitigate the severity of the famine. Tarasankar's works, however, apart from highlighting the effect of famine, venture to articulate the sociological consequence of it on human life where survival is the ultimate reality. "All his major characters have to accept the changes and adapt themselves to the new order of things because living is much more important than dying" (Devi 1969, 77).

The influence of social realism managed to transcend its boundary and penetrated the realm of painting. The art of colonial Bengal, which had long been celebrated by imperialists and nationalists alike, became limited to address the social situation caused by the economic havoc because of its traditional and classical predisposition. Famous artists of contemporary Bengal—like Jamini Roy, whose paintings represented a unique concoction of ancient Indian cave painting and Bengali Kalighat pot painting—often represented a stable household and repeatedly reinforced the gender roles of the society and hence became limited as a political weapon. Repulsion for fascism under an imperialist rule which had exacerbated the famine was, however, agathokakological in character. On the one hand, it took the lives of millions of Bengalis and forced them towards an ambiguous future. On the other hand, the influx of emaciated Bengali people to Calcutta for food not only created tremendous socio-economic instability but also managed to demystify the picturesqueness of Calcutta, thereby forcing the contemporary artists to step up for the social cause.

Political activism entwined with artistic creation gained steady momentum during the early 1940s, but a significant section of Bengali artists was undeterred by that contemporary trend. Nevertheless, an attempt to bring together works of artists without political affiliations as well as those affiliated to the Communist Party was taken up by the All India Student's Federation in 1944. As a result, the Bengal Painter's Testimony was published that consisted of a noteworthy number of artists whose content was the Bengal Famine. The publication had a moving forward written by Sarojini Naidu, where she urged people to buy the work by stating that the incredible contribution of the artists in portraying the devastation of the famine, the agony of the hungry and impoverished, with much honesty and clarity, would surely instigate the same feeling of sympathy from the Indian people. (Mallik 2001, 90) While the volume did not necessarily follow a strict theme based on the subject as well as the style and method of art, its main purpose was made clear in the editorial note, which was to raise funds (as each copy were sold at 5 rupees) and also to present the unity of artists across different social and religious strata. Therefore, the contributions of Indians alongside Europeans, as well as both Hindus and Muslims, were a conscious choice of the editors, rather than to focus on contributions of only famous artists in a bid to reduce the price of the book as well as to demonstrate patriotism and national unity. Additionally, the paintings of famous artists like Nandalal Bose, that were created well before the 1940s, were appropriated in the volume with different connotations and purposes. For instance, "one painting of Bose portrayed a skeleton-like figure of Lord Shiva dancing around the goddess Annapurna, the goddess of food, which consisted of a subtext written by Rabindranath Tagore where he described the art as a contradiction of the calmness against the Rudra dance, that broke the silence (Mallik 2001, 95). However, later in the volume, this quote was replaced with a quote by poet Bharatchandra, who mentioned this contradiction of the calm and the restlessness as "of having and not having of food(rice)" (Mallik 2001, 95).

A strong cultural protest movement against fascism that further intensified as a result of the famine had a strong Marxist inclination, as I have mentioned before. The fetish of the Bengali artists for social realism, however, was not merely a Marxist ideological import. It is undeniable that many artists during the late 1930s showed Marxist inclination and expressed their allegiance for leftist politics to use their respective art forms as a means of political mobilization rather than for sheer consumerism. The devastating effect of the Bengal famine ceased many artists from creating expensive art due to their poor economic conditions. Black and white sketches on the paper of poor quality, for many, was more of an economic choice rather than an ideological one. Moreover, several indigenous newspapers, regardless of their political affiliation, used sketches to report the contemporary situation, and hence lucidity over elusiveness was desired from the artists so that their message could fit perfectly with the newspaper report and leave hardly any room for the readers to interpret otherwise. With the exponential growth of political activities in Bengal, the party newspapers tried their best to match up with the situation by increasing the frequency of their publication of posters, news, and political propagandas where lack of party funds for printing and an increase in demand for political print compelled the artists to create artwork with minimum cost and within a very short amount of time (Ghosh 2013, 55).

One of these artists, whose minimalistic monochromatic sketches portrayed the horrific tragedy of the Bengal famine and led the contemporary colonial government to ban his work, was Chittoprasad Bhattacharya. Despite his artistic brilliance in portraying the reality of rural Bengal, his artwork was mostly limited to the Communist Party's political purposes and hence failed to elevate itself to the status of an elite art form. Like most of the artists and writers of his generation, his proclivity to social realism was not an anomaly. A Strong anti-fascist sentiment was triggered because of the potential fear of Japanese bombing in his home district of Chittagong, in modern-day Bangladesh. After the fall of Burma to the Japanese helped him find his voice that was recognized by the general secretary of the CPI, P.C Joshi. Within the cultural platform created by the CPI, the works of Chittoprasad became an important instrument in achieving that goal as his work made frequent appearances in the Communist Party's magazines like "People's War" and "Janayuddha." Chittoprasad, despite being an artist, adhered to the role of an activist, and hence in an interview, he unequivocally mentioned his artistic ethos by saying, "each artist must sooner or later, consciously or unconsciously, express his moral and political opinion. In my artwork, I represent the tradition of moralists and political reformers. To save people means to save art itself." He extensively traveled throughout rural Bengal and highlighted black-marketing, economic exploitation of the poor during the famine, and published his visual representation of the Bengal famine known as "Hungry Bengal: A Tour through Midnapore District." This volume was composed of written descriptions of his experience, which was supplemented by black and white sketches whose great anatomical detail consciously underscored the helpless expression of the skeleton-like bodies of rural Bengal.

Sanjukta Sunderson, in her work, correctly mentions that in Chittoprasad's work, "Hunger surfaces through these simplified lines not merely as a descriptive trope, but as evocative of emotional depletion as well. It is this psychological element in these drawings which integrates artistic imagination and empathy with investigation, moving beyond the immediate denotative element of journalistic illustration" (Sunderason 2011, 84). In 1943 he brilliantly captured the economic hardship of the people of Bengal through one of his sketches where a group of poverty-stricken people was shown to sell their belongings to a moneylender to feed their family. Similarly, one of his works depicted how few vultures were feeding on human bodies, an image that brilliantly portrayed the situation of the rural countryside during the infamous Bengal famine despite its grotesqueness. His social realism, therefore, was aimed at breaking the social alienation of the disillusioned contemporary Bengali middle-class. With his brutally honest sketches, he certainly tried to inflict extreme trauma among a section of the then society who, despite extreme socio-economic devastation, decided not to raise their voice against colonial rule.

The effect of Bengal famine was not restricted to the rural countryside of Bengal and certainly affected the colonial city of Calcutta, as was represented throughout the paintings of Zainul Abedin. Born in 1917, in East Bengal, the picturesqueness and natural abundance of his hometown initially attracted Zainul towards impressionism. The effect of famine, however, shifted his focus from impressionism to social realism. After completing his degree in 1938, he joined the government art college as a teacher, but the sudden social change caused by the famine compelled him to produce several artworks depicting the social evil of contemporary Bengal. Not only did he use rudimentary materials, but he also managed to portray the Bengal famine in a minimalistic yet horrific manner. Like Chittoprasad, his paintings left very little room for the viewers to interpret rather than commiserate, and he presented his subjects in a manner that highlighted the helplessness and despair of the poverty-stricken people of Bengal. One of his paintings depicted a hungry emaciated mother breastfeeding her famished child while another illustrated wasted skeleton-like bodies surrounded by ravens. His works also depicted how desperate with hunger the poor starving people were searching for food among discarded trash.

Conversely, as a result of the famine and other socio-political turmoil of the period, artistic development was not regulated by political parties. The rise of Fascism in Europe and Asia along with anti-imperial sentiments created a foundation for a different artistic expression that made a group of contemporary artists, independent of political affiliation, to go beyond the trajectory of Indian nationalist artistic style and embrace western artistic forms such as Expressionism and Cubism among others. This group of artists then formed the Calcutta Group, who was described by K.G. Subramanyan in his book "The Living Tradition," where he states, "[...] They belonged to the whole world, its language was their language; the Group opened itself out to the influence of the international idioms" (Mallik 2001, 142). While artists like Chittoprasad and Zainul Abedin featured documentary-style minimalist paintings, the Group addressed the Bengal Famine through experimental art forms as they believed that unlike the popularity of subjective artistic creations that were rigid in their interpretations, the people of India had the intellectual capacity to comprehend abstract art and interpret them in their ways. Moreover, the Group rejected any political affiliation so much so that they refused to denote themselves as "progressives," since the word had political implications associated with socialist ideals (Mallik 2001, 139). Within the Group, artists like Govardhan Ash, who joined in 1950, were moved to paint the mass exodus of the countryside to Calcutta from their personal experiences of the famine.

In these paintings, the subjects were presented more closely, with their fragile and destitute figures prominent, yet they seem to be fading away into oblivion, a metaphorical demonstration of the results of the famine. There were other artists of the Calcutta Group whose works, although coincided with the Bengal famine, never took a direct approach to portray the devastation. Artists such as Nirod Majumder and Prankrishmna Pal, whose paintings were created during the Bengal famine and appeared in Bengal Painter's testimony, certainly depicted human skeletal figures, but the farrago of Bengali pictorial tradition and European modernism distanced their work from any political representation. It was apparent that this group of Bengali artists, who had already established their eminence in their respective realms, was relatively protected from the harsh reality of contemporary Bengal, but felt the moral obligation to deliberately step forward during the crisis deliberately by not challenging the colonial authority.

In concluding my essay, I would like to state that I have consciously limited the number of literary, artistic, and dramatic representations of Bengali writers and artists due to the limited scope of the publication. The 1940s was a crucial period for the world and in Bengal, the impact of the famine gave social activists and literary associations a new sense of responsibility and a renewed spirit to fight years of colonial subjugation. However, the growing influence of the CPI, despite its political limitations, over the works of their members grew with time so much so that by the end of the 1950s, many left the party as it constricted their artistic creations and freedom of expression. Nevertheless, the transformation in the art and literary culture of Bengal that was catapulted by the Bengal famine of 1943 became an ongoing process, as challenges to the earlier ways of living gave way to new forms of livelihood for the Bengali people, which moved the society further towards collective resistance against colonial rule.

References

Devereux, Stephen. 2001. "Sen's Entitlement Approach: Critiques and Counter-Critiques." *Oxford Development Studies* 29, no. 3: pp. 245-263. [doi: 10.1080/13600810120088859]

Devi, Mahasweta. 1969. "Tarashankar's World of Changes and the New Order." *Indian Literature* 12, no. 1: pp. 71-79.

Ghosh, Chilka. 2013. "Visual Art, Realism and the Issue of Taste: Marxist Cultural Debates in the 1940s." *Social Scientist* 41, no. 3-4: pp. 49-64.

Mallik, Sanjoy K. 2001. *Developments in the modern art of Bengal since 1940s: Volume 1.* Baroda: Maharaja Sayajirao University of Baroda.

Mitra, Sarojmohan. 1979-1980. "Progressive Cultural Movement in Bengal." *Social Scientist* 8, no. 5-6: pp. 115-120.

Mukherjee, Arunkumar. 1975. "Bibhutibhusan and Manik Bandyopadhyay." *Indian Literature* 18, no. 4: pp. 32-40.

Panikkar, K. N. 2011. "Progressive Cultural Movement in India: A Critical Appraisal." *Social Scientist* 39, no. 11-12: pp. 14-25.

Sunderason, Sanjukta. 2011. "As Agitator and Organiser: Chittaprasad and Art for the Communist Party of India, 1941-1948." *Object,* no.13: pp. 76-95.

Chapter 7

Commodifying Trumpian Propaganda: *The Grifter Art of Jon McNaughton**

Nat Hardy, Ph.D. M.F.A., FRSA

Stephens College, USA

Abstract

This chapter explores how Jon McNaughton's Trumpian portraiture propaganda sustains a hyper-myopic focus on the cult of personality of President Donald J. Trump for the dual purposes of public notoriety and private financial gain. To McNaughton's credit, the art-for-profit craftsman has established a lucrative niche market, capitalizing off of a burgeoning congregation of non-elite art lovers, who, like Fox News' Sean Hannity, seek to adorn their walls with framed or unframed portraits of McNaughton's growing catalog of Pro-Trump-Meets-Tea-Party "authoritarian kitsch."

In deconstructing McNaughton's growing catalog of cult of personality paintings, this chapter demonstrates that despite the artist's denials, this Trumpian purveyor of hyper-patriotism exposes a post-truth Norman Rockwell-esque mercenary cashing in on what Hannah Arendt described as "propaganda thriv[ing] on this escape from reality into fiction." To this end, McNaughton's glorified renderings of Trump are political spectacles that personify and celebrate the President's narcissistic and despotic temperaments. As propaganda paintings, McNaughton's political works traffic in disinformation and indoctrination — the manipulation of the naïve and willing MAGA masses through iron-fisted didacticism and fanatical tableaus of delusion.

But perhaps McNaughton's modus operandi explains his lucrative success best; his uncanny ability to create appealing and triumphal Trumpian

* This chapter was written by the author before the celebration of the Presidential Elections in the US, which took place on November 3rd, 2020. The winner of the elections was Joe Biden. Donald Trump contested that the results were suspicious of electoral fraud because of the vote-by-mail system.

demagogical scenes, and peddle his works within a profitable online matrix where art meets mass-market propaganda ideologically hand-crafted for collectors and end consumers.

Keywords: Christian Nationalism; McNaughton; opportunism; propaganda; theocratic tribalism;

* * *

For the sophisticated gatekeepers of the American art world, the artist Jon McNaughton, one of "the premiere French Barbizon Impressionist[s]" (Mormon Wiki 2020) painting today, might never appear in the hallowed pages of Janson's History of Art; not because of the artist's demonstrated abilities, but likely on account of his often volatile mytho-political content. Nevertheless, within the aesthetic gaze of the Neoconservative Christian Right, McNaughton is hailed as "America's painter" for "Making Art Great Again" in post-truth America.[1] As the nation's "most famous pro-Trump mass-market painter of the twenty-first century" (Hesse 2018), this purveyor of propaganda refers to himself as a "political" (Weist 2018) and a "historical painter" (Hesse 2018), or, as McNaughton self-describes the incendiary nature of his art: "When I paint a patriotic painting," he notes, "It's like throwing a stick of dynamite in the pond!" (Hastings 2012). As his explosive metaphor implies, McNaughton's politically weaponized paintings are completely void of any subtlety and purposely composed to evoke strong responses from viewers; whether positively or negatively. As visual rhetoric then, McNaughton uses shock and awe imagery to inflame and inspire his audience not only to react to his intemperate works, but, in the end, to convert his MAGA audience from admirer-to-consumer to consumer-to-purchaser.

Although McNaughton uses the entire spectrum of the color wheel and a diverse blend of pigments in his political paintings, as an extreme right-wing artist and propagandist, he inhabits a monochromatic ideological world where there are no shades of grey, only a black-and-white realm tinted with greenbacks—or, as the Christian Nationalist might say: the "almighty" dollar. In McNaughton and Trump's either/or fallacious realms, there is only radical right-wing "right"—all competing or opposing political, meaning "left," positions are "wrong."[2] As a right-wing partisan, McNaughton paints political portraits not for art's sake, but to promote and exacerbate the growing political

[1] In 2018, artist Justin Lieberman advocated that the U.S. State Department should have Jon McNaughton represent America at the Venice Biennale. (Dafoe 2018)

[2] Like Trump again, McNaughton labels their left-wing adversaries as: "Socialist," "Marxist," "Antifa," "Deep State," "Liberal," and "Democrat," among others.

divisions that Trump continues to sew and promote. In this sense, McNaughton's approach to his propaganda portraits is—like Trump's world of alternative facts—agnotological at its core.

While McNaughton demonstrates artistic talent, he is considered by many critics and detractors as a "hack" artist, motivated by radical-right Christian politics and by the McNaughton Fine Arts Company's profit margin. Taking the need to express his ideology and biases through propaganda paintings for populist ends and fiscal benefits, McNaughton's target market is Conservative-Christian Republicans. Thus, it is within this marketplace of Grand Old Party ideas and chauvinistic consumerism that McNaughton and his kindred comrades connect. Through his boilerplate artworks, McNaughton cannot only freely express his adoration of an incompetent and increasingly authoritarian leader through fantasy and deception, but he can be handsomely compensated for his print and canvas venerations if his fans click-to-purchase a Trumpian-inspired item from his online storefront; with "Shopping Cart Software by Bigcommerce" (McNaughton 2020).

As a purveyor of visual "product," and, as the loaded images align with the values and patriotic fantasies of the Trump administration and its supporters, the entrepreneurial artist has rather skillfully market-positioned his growing operation. McNaughton's brand identity is unparalleled, and his growing catalog of best-selling "patriotic" wares—where Barbizon-meets-Bizarre—are, without question, out of the ordinary. And while McNaughton's artworks of Donald Trump likely inspire his right-wing MAGA (Make America Great Again) audience to embrace Trump's cult of personality on canvas, as propaganda, artistic intention is patently obvious[3]—there is no mystery or ambiguity in his imagery—only pomposity and hard-nose trumpery at retail prices (plus shipping and taxes).

Mirroring his Mormon roots in many ways, McNaughton's aesthetic has neither wavered nor evolved as he has matured. Throughout his entire body of work to date, McNaughton has remained a firmly entrenched realist painter, or, as Rod Dreher, the senior editor of *The American Conservative*, describes McNaughton: he is the "Titian of Trumpian realism" (Dreher 2018). While there may be Titian elements in his paintings, McNaughton's realist style has been described as "French Barbizon Impressionism" (Mormon Wiki 2020). Indeed, of all right-wing propaganda artists working in contemporary America today,

---

[3] As McNaughton maintains: "I started painting patriotic art because it allows me to express my frustrations in ways I cannot do with words," it seems contradictory that if the artist "paints in words," why does he explain, in great detail, each painting in print and in videos? (Rees 2012)

few, if any, compare to this incendiary painter known as "the Right's Shepherd Fairey" (Wolfe 2012), America's "Tea Party Painter," (Morgan 2012) and "the Thomas Kinkade of Mormonism" (Oliaz and Duffy 2011); an artist whose "dramatic fusion of Christian piety and conservative ideology" (Rees 2012) remains largely mocked by the mainstream artworld for his clownish pro-Trump propaganda paintings.

This chapter will explore how McNaughton's Trumpian portraiture propaganda sustains a hyper-myopic focus on the cult of personality of President Donald J. Trump for the dual purposes of public notoriety and private financial gain. To McNaughton's credit, the art-for-profit craftsman has established a lucrative niche market, capitalizing off of a burgeoning congregation of non-elite art lovers, who, like Fox News' Sean Hannity, seek to adorn their walls with framed or unframed portraits of McNaughton's growing catalog of Pro-Trump-Meets-Tea-Party "authoritarian kitsch" (Substack 2009).

McNaughton's critics have categorized his paintings through a wide variety of genres, including "pure propaganda" (McDonald 2020), "Capitalist Realism" (Dreher 2018), "political cartoon" (Jamitis 2018), "bad academic derivative realism" (Shapiro 2012), and as "more ideogram than objet d'art" (Morgan 2012). As an armchair art critic, I would add a few additional generic categories, including social realism, fabulist realism, retrofuturism, shock art, and political iconography, in an attempt to characterize McNaughton's eclectic Barbizonian aesthetic. This compound blend of creative approaches enables McNaughton to create a Trumpian mythos of a political everyman—a devout Christian—and a tough, authoritarian protector. As Jim Jamitis suggests, however, McNaughton's unsubtle "art is Trump hero worship delivered on a brickbat. It is idolatry" (Jamitis 2018). Unlike abstract propaganda art, such as Picasso's Guernica (1937)—which requires interpretation and context to fully comprehend or simply derive pleasure from—"the Picasso of Provo's" (Shapiro 2012) realist propaganda paintings require no interlocutor. If anything, McNaughton is a master of overstatement, which is blatantly evidenced through his iconic renderings celebrating authoritarian white nationalism and painstakingly detailed in oil and acrylic-based "colors that don't run." While McNaughton's works are "technically competent" (Tait 2019), as Jim Jamitis points out, "politically-motivated art is usually bad art. It spoon-feeds an obvious message requiring not thought on the part of the person viewing the art" (Jamitis 2018).

Throughout Western history, most, if not all, from ancient-to-modern monarchs and dictators have employed defenders: writers, painters, sculptors and photographers in order to enhance the leader's status and to reinforce authoritarian messaging through deception and rhetorical subterfuge. In the grand scheme of things, of course, McNaughton's fanciful, hyper-patriotic works are simply part of a new entry in the burgeoning encyclopedia of visual propaganda, a political tradition that can be traced back to ancient Egyptian, Greek and Roman times. While the more dominant medium of statuary was the preferred method for propaganda for the ancients, during the Renaissance, oil painting would prove to be the ideal medium for conveying supreme political power. Taking his lead from a long tradition of propaganda art then, McNaughton's genre paintings are contrived in what Jeb Substack appropriately describes as "a heroically muscular pastiche of neoclassical-fascist and socialist realism" (Substack 2019). And although the McNaughton Fine Art Company's website does not directly allude to "partisan" or "propaganda" paintings, it does have a category of "Conservative Drawings" (McNaughton 2020) where Trump is featured prominently.

While Napoleon Bonaparte was lionized by Jacques-Louis David in the nineteenth century, Donald Trump has Jon McNaughton to help mythologize the American President as the twenty-first century's autocratic and messianic president. As his flowering catalog illustrates, McNaughton continues to immortalize Trump in a variety of over-the-top heroic roles, including great emancipator (You Are Not Forgotten, McNaughton 2020), pious leader (National Emergency, McNaughton 2020), artistic genius (The Masterpiece, McNaughton 2020), staunch defender of truth (You Are Fake News, McNaughton 2020), allegorical sage (Teach a Man to Fish, McNaughton 2020), passionate patriot (Respect the Flag), gridiron champion (All American Trump, McNaughton 2020), champion rodeo bull rider (2020 Ride, McNaughton 2020), the nation's protector (Make America Safe, McNaughton 2020), biker (MAGA Ride, McNaughton 2020), a postmodern George Washington (Crossing the Swamp, McNaughton 2020), a machismo bully (Expose the Truth, McNaughton 2020), and the greatest American president ever (Trump Rushmore, McNaughton 2020). In deconstructing McNaughton's growing catalog of cult of personality paintings, this chapter will demonstrate that despite the artist's denials, this Trumpian purveyor of hyper-patriotism exposes a post-truth Norman Rockwell-esque mercenary cashing in on what Hannah Arendt described as "propaganda thriv[ing] on this escape from reality into fiction" (Arendt 1958, 352). Of course, in addition to McNaughton's iconic hagiographic Trump portraits, the artist also has an affinity for promoting deep-state conspiracy theories, as evidenced in Obamanation (McNaughton 2020) and Expose the Truth (McNaughton 2020).

While propagandist art is not a new genre, indeed, with the advent of the internet, the creation and dissemination of agitprop art have become, to use the modern vernacular: "viral." While largely anonymous photoshop artists create pro bono political memes for circulation on social media, Jon McNaughton earns a handsome profit creating politico-religious propaganda paintings for the right-wing cult worship market of Donald J. Trump and—with less frequency—Jesus. As John Perticone suggests: “McNaughton doesn't care about the haters, he just wants to paint Trump and Jesus” (Perticone 2018). While McNaughton's growing number of renderings of the 45th President cast Trump as a “Christian Warrior” (Cole 2019), who, as Trump himself asserts, “is above the law” (Rodgers 2020), Trump's warrior persona echoes that of the King of Kings who “came not to abolish the law, but to fulfill it” (Matthew 5:18). In keeping with McNaughton's Trump/Jesus Complex, both of McNaughton's messianic characters are represented by the artist in a didactic dualism: god-like patriots and/or pious victims. As “righteous” leaders, Trump and Jesus also share a common capacity for vengeance and violence. Jesus, for example, confesses in Matthew 10:34: “Do not suppose that I have come to bring peace to the earth. I did not come to bring peace, but a sword,” and, as McNaughton proclaims of Trump: “They [non-Trump supporters] may have the power to bruise his [Trump's] heel, but he [Trump] will have the power to crush their head!” (McNaughton 2020).

While the ancient Greeks had the sacred nine muses for artistic inspiration, McNaughton is obsessed with two: Donald J. Trump and Jesus Christ (in that order). While a virtual army of Conservative Christian artists has flooded the internet with photoshopped imagery of Trump and Jesus together, the deific duo has yet to appear simultaneously in one of McNaughton's paintings. Knowing McNaughton's devotion and adoration of this “Christian” president and the proliferation of Trump/Jesus depictions on the web, however, such imagery is very likely forthcoming. Moreover, the subtext of McNaughton's messianic associations between the two powerful prophet/profit spirits is unambiguous, as the painter celebrates and reveres “The Lord of Lords” and the “Lord of Landlords” on canvas. In the artist's defense, however, McNaughton's Trumpian renderings are in keeping with the President's hubristic claim: “I am the chosen one” (Milbank 2019). Indeed, between the evangelical support for the President and Trump's persistent legal attempts and successes at eliminating Jefferson's “wall of separation between church and state” (Baker 2018), McNaughton's sanctimonious portrayals of the President, by no accident, cast the President in “godly” company. Through this didactic blend of Christian Nationalism and “folksy fascism” (Zoom 2018), McNaughton creates an American messiah that appeals to Trump's evangelical base, as demonstrated in You Are Not Forgotten, which depicts “Trump as a Messiah figure, depicting the President standing on the head of a snake—an obvious allusion to messianic prophecy in Genesis 3:15” (Jamitis 2018).

As advertised on his rather vast online inventory, McNaughton's works are notorious for consolidating church and state, not only because conjoining the two institutions reflects the artist's commitment to Christian Nationalism, but because McNaughton argues that the assimilation makes for the finest art possible. As McNaughton explains: "If you mix politics and religion in painting ... it makes you think and feel it is the greatest art of all!" (Rees 2012). While McNaughton's aesthetic philosophy is open to debate, the artist's wholesale rejection of church/state separation is not. As a Republican theocrat, McNaughton continues to demonstrate a deep-seated passion for inextricably linking Trump and Jesus as pious intercessors as both One Nation Under God (McNaughton 2020) and You Are Not Forgotten (McNaughton 2020) attest. And while an American president might rule the nation from the oval office, for a Mormon like McNaughton, ultimately, it is Jesus who must inhabit the throne of government, which is best exemplified in his "masterpiece," One Nation Under God (McNaughton 2020), where a pasty-white Jesus appears hand-delivering the U.S. Constitution to deserving, god-fearing Americans. The political theosophy here illustrates the notion that Christ is America's as the supreme Founding Father. As a theocratic image, One Nation Under God, of course, in keeping with McNaughton's belief in the Church of Jesus Christ of the Latter-Day Saints' position that the Constitution was "divinely inspired" (Perry 1976).

In stark contrast to McNaughton's Jesus-as-King, Separation of Church and State (McNaughton 2020) is a theocracy-under-attack mise en scène that portrays Jesus-as-outcast during a State of the Union Address. In this painting, McNaughton imagines Jesus being banished from the Congressional Chamber by a "godless" Congress. As McNaughton explains: "The painting is meant to be a symbol of our government's abandonment of God and His Covenant" (McNaughton 2020). Thus, even though the United States was founded as—and remains—a secular nation, through a combination of McNaughton's revisionism and fringe theology, McNaughton maintains that America, despite appearances, is an intolerant and unapologetic theocracy. In a Twitter rant promoting Separation of Church and State, McNaughton explains his inspiration for his pièce de résistance: "I've had enough of Jesus Christ being kicked out of everything, replaced by LGTBQ and Islamic propaganda. When push comes to shove, American Christians will stand for their rights," (@McNaughtonArt, July 29, 2018) unless of course, they are kneeling in prayer as they are wont to do, in one of McNaughton's many of his worship-inspired paintings.

With respect to McNaughton's allusions to the LGBTQ community and appeals to Islamophobia, it seems ambiguous as to whether McNaughton is promoting church/state or church/hate values. Perhaps both. As McNaughton bemoans, it is "the Separation of Church and State... [that] protects Buddhists, and Muslims and Atheists today." (McNaughton 2020) Moreover, like McNaughton's own Islamophobia, anti-LGTBQ policies and propaganda are core values of his fellow passengers on the Trump Train and a signature theme for his ardent supporters. Take, for example, a pro-Trump Kentucky BBQ food truck that sells "I Support LGBTQ: Liberty, Guns, Bible, Trump & BBQ" (Castrodale 2019) t-shirts at a brisk pace.

In keeping with McNaughton's theocratic impulses, in And Justice for All (McNaughton 2020), the artist paints his own challenge to the Establishment Clause of the First Amendment and the rule of secular law. In this divinely-inspired spectacle, McNaughton foregrounds Moses and the Ten Commandments in front of the U.S. Supreme Court Building. To connect the biblical lawgiver with the American people, Moses is accompanied by a cast of, according to McNaughton, "American Heroes" from the "founding" of the nation through to the present "floundering" of the nation. As McNaughton says of the painting: "Let us always endeavor to be a nation of laws and of God, never of man" (McNaughton 2020). Thus, if the imagery does not visually convey America as a theocracy, the artist's messaging certainly does. Similarly, McNaughton's The Empowered Man (McNaughton 2020)—a pre-Trump tour de force—presents a defiant Republican Joe Six-Pack seizing the Constitution from the clutches of the "godless" politicians assembled in the background. Alas, American theocracy triumphs once again.

As a devout Mormon artist, McNaughton's visual rhetoric might appear outlandish on occasion; nevertheless, his foundational thesis remains consistent that "America is a Christian Nation," a revisionist sentiment shared by another vocal supporter of President Trump, Televangelist Robert Jeffress of the First Baptist Church in Dallas (Montgomery 2020). Like Trump, the Texan preacher has accumulated considerable wealth—$17 million—(The Wealth Record 2020), not bad for "a man of God." Of course, it follows that a wealthy Christian Nation requires a tough, Christian businessman. If there is one thing McNaughton and Jeffress agree on, it is that Donald Trump is a Conservative Christian demigod, even in spite of Trump's recorded business failures, unpaid bills, bankruptcies, and two divorces. Within Trump's and Jeffress' world of alternative facts, however, McNaughton continues to disseminate and celebrate the revisionist myth that Trump is both a successful businessman and a god-fearing Christian. Of course, creating Trumpian art makes McNaughton a wealthy businessman and a godly Mormon as well.

To further underscore McNaughton's theocratic insistence for consolidating religion in the affairs of state, McNaughton markets portrays three seemingly devout and supplicating presidents on bended knees in Washington's Prayer (McNaughton 2020), Lincoln's Prayer (McNaughton 2020), and in the wildly anachronistic The Empowered Man (McNaughton 2020), where James Madison appears transfixed in a euphoric invocation. Of course, Madison seems an odd choice to promote theocracy, given the fact that "Madison famously rejected any religious sanction for government authority" (Knight 2012). Nevertheless, McNaughton's most recent praying president is, predictably, Donald Trump, who—unlike McNaughton's other praying Commanders-in-Chief—stands in prayer in a painting entitled National Emergency (McNaughton 2020). In this curious portrait, Trump's erect pose is deliberate. The President's upright position is indicative of his hubris—a President who believes he is "the greatest American President ever"—"stands" tall above the kneeling Washington, Madison, and Lincoln. Since kneeling is "a posture of expressing humility" (Encyclopedia Britannica 2020), meekness is a character trait for other presidents, not Donald J. Trump. Clearly, Trump is supplicant for no one: Man or God, a self-absolving position confirmed by the President's insistence that he has never asked God's forgiveness for his sins (Tani 2016).

In a just-released painting, Legacy of Hope (McNaughton 2020), an array of historical characters surrounds Trump, who is seated at a table praying. On that table in front of the President lay a set of skeleton keys, the Bible and a Constitution. Like magic, Ronald Reagan, George Washington, and Abraham Lincoln appear touching President Trump's shoulders while the other characters pray along in unison. And while it would be difficult to imagine that Martin Luther King Jr., John F. Kennedy, Frederick Douglass, and Harriet Tubman would be Trump supporters—given the current President's policies and prejudices—they too appear in the painting, praying in support of the 45th President, along with, incidentally, the Confederate General, Robert E. Lee. Again, although the President is not standing in prayer as he does in National Emergency, in Legacy of Hope Trump is seated and not kneeling in humility.

Beyond aggrandizing praying presidents, McNaughton features other righteous characters, such as a family praying in front of an American flag in Mending the Nation (McNaughton 2020), and in Pray for America (McNaughton 2020), which features a head-bowed cowboy on horseback, clutching a flag in one hand and hat in the other. And while collection plates are conspicuously absent in McNaughton's religiously-inspired paintings, mercantile charity is always welcomed by McNaughton Fine Arts Company, as the storefront accepts all major credit cards, including PayPal and Coupon Codes,[4] as well. Thus, while their profitable strategies might diverge, what truly unites McNaughton, Trump and Jeffress, is the ability to capitalize off of the evangelical fusion of church and state. Indeed, as history reminds us, the Republican appeal to evangelicals helped Trump win the 2016 election, it has enabled Jeffress to become a multi-millionaire, and the pictorial merging of

---

[4] Available at couponxxo.com.

church and state has granted McNaughton the opportunity to win the hearts, minds, and wallets of Trumpists throughout the nation.

As a footnote, it bears noting, however, that before McNaughton descended into the bathetic depths of propagandist art, the early-career artist enjoyed a rather benign, albeit profitable career painting Kinkadian-like landscapes and saccharine religious scenes. However, during the tenure of former President Barack Obama, the sentimental inklings that once pervaded his work had radically changed, and McNaughton's art took a decidedly and overtly hard-right theocratic tone as Obama and the Democratic Party had become McNaughton's legislative muses.

To provide some context as to how McNaughton's art evolved from the "deep-seated hatred of President Obama" (Hastings 2012) to the Cult of Personality of Donald Trump, it is appropriate to give some pre-Trump background. With the ascension of Donald Trump to the presidency, McNaughton shifted his focus to the 45th President with fanatical abandon, but prior to 2016, McNaughton dedicated his creative energies to producing a series of his anti-Obama paintings, which include The Forgotten Man (McNaughton 2020), The Empowered Man (McNaughton 2020), The Demise of America (McNaughton 2020), Obamanation (McNaughton 2020), One Nation Under Socialism (McNaughton 2020), Obama Foreign Policy (McNaughton 2020), and Wake Up America (McNaughton 2020), "which critics say [are] animated by racial bias" (Hastings 2012). Where McNaughton's grandiose Trumpian portraits are unapologetically intended to rally partisan support for the President, the Obama paintings aim to inflame and inspire hatred and disdain of the 44th President through racism and demonization vis-à-vis Obama's political and ideological left-leaning affiliation. While McNaughton exudes confidence in his unwavering beliefs, the artist, on rare occasions, conveys self-criticism. As McNaughton says of One Nation Under Socialism (McNaughton 2020), a painting that features Obama burning the Constitution, for example: "When I painted it, I worried, this thing is just hideous — why would anybody hang that in their living room?" (Hesse 2018).

While demonizing political enemies and a free press is a time-honored tradition in propaganda, McNaughton casts liberals in a malignant light, which is best exemplified in his painting, Liberalism is a Disease (McNaughton 2020), a painting that Jonny Coleman of LA Weekly characterizes as one of the most "atrocious examples of American Conservative Art" (Coleman 2017). Similarly, McNaughton's National Emergency (McNaughton 2020) features a cadre of Democrats standing on the American flag, while Speaker Pelosi and Chuck Schumer hold the Mexican flag. As McNaughton writes, in the background are the "Dangerous drug smugglers, human traffickers, and other criminals" (McNaughton 2020) pouring across the border, while the Democrats celebrate and cheer the border surgers on. McNaughton's The Impeachment Mob (McNaughton 2020), much like its title suggests, presents a vengeful pack of obviously out-for-blood, leading Democrats, along with Republican Mitt Romney, holding torches, pitchforks, boards, baseball bats. Rather predictably, McNaughton's crowning Meisterstück foregrounds Adam Schiff foisting the Liberal lynch mob's noose. These rather ham-fisted examples—and there are others—are indicative of McNaughton's penchant for intolerance and insistence for overstatement, and as John McDonald suggests: "McNaughton's work is pure propaganda, pushing a homegrown mythology that reinforces all the Trump positives and ignores the negatives, but it will not convince the President's detractors" (McDonald 2020).

As propaganda art, McNaughton's visual rhetoric engages in a range of fallacies in each of his works. The most prominent fallacy McNaughton indulges in is the design fallacy, an artifice which persuades his audience that because he has invested considerable time, effort and skill to produce his Trumpian portraits, that, at least to MAGA supporters are aesthetically pleasing, such investment and craftmanship lends veracity—no matter how fantastical—to the imagery. Additionally, artistic license and McNaughton's penchant for bootlicking sycophancy enable the artist to make Trump appear 30-40 pounds lighter. In a similar fashion, the President's trademark orange spray tan—courtesy of McNaughton's brushstrokes—fades into a much more natural tan. Somewhat like photoshop, the oil-based medium also provides McNaughton with unrivaled poetic license; indeed, the only restriction is the predictable scope of McNaughton's unbridled right-wing political imagination. As demonstrated in his growing repertoire, McNaughton has the talent and inventiveness to portray Trump in a range of mytho-heroic roles—a league of one extraordinary gentleman—if you will.

In a long tradition of artists glorifying authoritarian despots from Western history then, McNaughton serves in a similar capacity as President Trump's self-appointed "Court Evangelical and... Court artist" (Fea 2019), an opportunist motivated by personal profit and wholly devoted to promoting Trump's political agenda through a growing catalog of oil-based fantasies. To this end, McNaughton's glorified renderings of Trump are political spectacles that personify and celebrate the President's narcissistic and despotic temperaments. As propaganda paintings, McNaughton's political works traffic in disinformation and indoctrination—the manipulation of the naïve and willing MAGA masses through iron-fisted didacticism and fanatical tableaus of delusion—as best exemplified in McNaughton's You Are Not Forgotten (McNaughton 2020). As McNaughton conveys in the "Product Description" for the painting: "I want a president to crush the enemies of liberty, justice, and American prosperity" (McNaughton 2020). To his entrepreneurial credit,

McNaughton's portraits exude Trumpian Weltanschauung in all its dogmatic and commercial glory and target marketed to an adoring MAGA audience.

Since the 2016 presidential election, McNaughton has become the darling of the MAGA movement and a best-selling artist because his propaganda paintings attract Trump supporters through a creative montage of celebratory, combative and defiant portrayals of the 45th president. "The people who buy [McNaughton's] paintings are buying [them]," as Monica Hesse suggests, "because the message seems to be, "#MAGA #MAGA #MAGA," in big neon lights" (Hesse 2018). Through idolatrous imagery and market appeal to a captive audience, McNaughton seizes on a timely range of Trumpian triumphs, scandals, and fantasies that are best exemplified in one of his most recent works, Trump Rushmore (McNaughton 2020). Moreover, in case a viewer might miss one of McNaughton's Trumpian allusions, gaslightings, or dog whistles, each artwork is explained in print and in video in painstaking detail on the McNaughton Art Company website. And while many artists compose manifestos to explain their aesthetic approach and their craft, for each of his works, McNaughton composes verbal propaganda to accompany his visual propaganda.

From aesthetic and pecuniary perspectives, the inspiration behind Jon McNaughton's burgeoning catalog can be characterized as a hybrid confluence of two other commercially-successful American painters: Thomas Kinkade and Norman Rockwell. Just as Donald Trump is never short of hubris, McNaughton describes himself on The McNaughton Fine Arts Company website as "America's Painter" (McNaughton 2020), an epithet long-associated with none other than the iconic Norman Rockwell. Additionally, McNaughton also credits James Michael Pratt, an author and filmmaker, for making the McNaughton/Rockwell connection. "When I first saw Jon McNaughton's patriotic, faith, and Americana art," claims Pratt, "I thought of Norman Rockwell and knew he [McNaughton] was America's Artist for our current generation and crisis" (McNaughton 2020). Rather fittingly, both McNaughton's and Pratt's association fallacies are united in their obvious attempts to elevate the propagandist's status among the annals of other notable American artists. Beyond fallacy, however, Rockwell's and McNaughton's work are more divergent than similar, particularly with respect to artistic intent. "McNaughton's work is often compared to that of Norman Rockwell due to its realism and patriotic themes," as Aaron Gell argues, however, "where Rockwell was characterized by a heartwarming folksiness — lending even highly charged political issues, like the battles over civil rights, a gauzy sense of reassurance — McNaughton takes a more polemical approach" (Gell 2017).

For many of McNaughton's growing cadre of critics, most Rockwell/McNaughton comparisons are less than flattering. For example, McNaughton, an avid promoter of his own works on Twitter, is frequently cited on the social media platform, leading two Twitter users to describe the controversial artist as a "Nazi Norman Rockwell" (@MollyJongFasy, May 1, 2009) and "Norman Reichwell" (@UncleRamrod, May 2, 2009). And where Rockwell's many paintings for The Saturday Evening Post covers were highly original, McNaughton is prone to plagiarizing famous artworks as he does in Crossing the Swamp (McNaughton 2020), wherein a cast of Republican characters paddle their way across an imaginary Washington, D.C. swamp, complete with alligators. In this portrait, McNaughton appropriates Emanuel Leutze's Washington Crossing the Delaware (1851). In The Resistance (McNaughton 2020), McNaughton channels Francisco de Goya's The Third of May, 1808, replacing the execution of Spanish rebels by French troops with MAGA supporters being clubbed to death by an Antifa mob who warm themselves by the flames from the burning Stars and Stripes.

Given McNaughton's preoccupation with social realism, capitalism and communism collide when comparing McNaughton's The Masterpiece (McNaughton 2020) with Isaak Brodsky's V.I. Lenin and Manifestation (1919) (Uglow 2017). In The Masterpiece, Trump appears painting in a cathedral,[5] and like some artistic Wizard of Oz, the President partially pulls back a maroon cover to reveal his next political masterstroke (although it is unclear what canvas will reveal, owing to the red draping obscuring the portrait). While Brodsky's composition does not portray Lenin as an artist, like Trump, Lenin appears pulling back a crimson curtain to reveal a revolutionary demonstration in the square below. As actual and aspiring autocrats, both leaders rule in revolutionary times. For Lenin, it was a communist revolution, and for Trump, it is a cultural revolution. In The Con Artist (McNaughton 2020), McNaughton abandons his Russian influence for a Norwegian muse—Edvard Munch—as he portrays Hillary Rodham Clinton in a poorly pilfered version of The Scream (1893). And in a final insult to mimesis, McNaughton takes caricature to an even further parodic level, as his painting Democrats Playing Poker (McNaughton 2020) plagiarizes Cassius Coolidge's kitsch painting Dogs Playing Poker (1894) (Taggart 2018).

Like Thomas Kinkade, a devout Christian whose inspiration, so he claimed, derived from his faith, the early-career McNaughton also continues to paint bucolic and pastoral landscapes, as well as religious scenes, that is when he is not creating Trumpian portraits. Unlike Kinkade's popular depictions of the Christian faith, which typically consist of churches and crosses on scenic hills,

---

[5] In this somewhat subtle allusion, McNaughton, once again, emphasizes Trump-as-Christian President, and as a theocrat — the unification of church and state — as Trump is clearly working in a cathedral.

however, the radical-right McNaughton departs from Kinkade's passive Arcadianism, as much of McNaughton's propaganda catalog is devoted to the reactionary mixing of politics and religion through hard-boiled proselytism and "folksy fascism" (Zoom 2018). As a Twitter user, @sadhourglass put it: McNaughton's art is an "attempt to combine photorealism and Impressionism like a bastardization of Thomas Kinkade" (@sadhourglass, February 26, 2018).

While there may be some similarities with respect to technique and execution, McNaughton and Kinkade wholly diverge concerning content. Where Kinkade was a "Painter of Light," "the Thomas Kinkade of Mormonism" (Oliaz and Duffy 2011) is a propaganda painter whose myopic focus is muckraking, conspiracy theories, and right-wing evangelism. And while both artists profit handsomely from their works, where Kinkade created homespun, apolitical landscapes, McNaughton indulges in painting political and populist landmines that explode off the canvas.

What McNaughton does have in common with Thomas Kinkade is a successful art-for-profit business. As a prosperous entrepreneur, McNaughton is cashing in on a burgeoning demand for populist art through his own particular "MAPA" (Make Art Profitable Again) talent to exploit the MAGA market. In the spirit of "MAPA," the McNaughton Fine Arts Company has its own marketing and promotions team, as illustrated on the company's website. Indeed, for this artist/merchant, McNaughton's works are not even listed as "art" or "paintings," but rather as "products." Beyond McNaughton's in-house promotions, the artist is actively networking to improve his company's bottom line where painting prices (whether original or print) can be sorted on his website from "Bestselling," "Low to High," or "High to Low."

While Rockwell's "Americana" paintings are often rhetorical, and in some instances, propagandistic, Rockwell was prone to employing humor and wit in his classic magazine covers. In stark contrast to Rockwell, McNaughton's propaganda portraits consistently project a humorless and ironfisted cult of personality. As R.C. Baker suggests of the aesthetic juxtaposition: "McNaughton has been compared to Norman Rockwell, and while both artists painted for reproduction (Rockwell for magazine covers, McNaughton for giclée prints), the comparison falls flat" (Baker 2018). Moreover, while "Rockwell was often working on tight deadlines ... it is McNaughton's work that feels rushed" (Baker 2018).

Perhaps McNaughton's most rushed and slap-dashed works appeared just days after Trump's July 4th, 2020 rally. With the paint still drying, Trump Rushmore (McNaughton 2020) was offered for retail at the "where-art-meets-retail" McNaughton Fine Arts Company. For McNaughton—time is of the essence—the enterprising businessman-within-the-artist understands the need to strike while the iron is hot because the Trump Rushmore moment is just that. Within a week of launching Trump Rushmore, McNaughton released two new paintings for sale on his website: The Choice and Legacy of Hope (McNaughton 2020). This assembly-line approach to painting is, of course, consistent with McNaughton's formula for business success: maintain cultural currency in order to increase sales. Of course, once another occasion to celebrate Trump transpires, Trump Rushmore may end up in the McNaughton Fine Art's Company bargain bin, or featured in one of the artist's repackaged "Patriot Packs," to make way for the next hagiographic installment of the 45th President.[6]

Just as Trump used the media during the 2016 election to promote himself, McNaughton cleverly garners free advertising to promote The McNaughton Fine Art Company's prints and paintings. Indeed, before McNaughton was commercially successful, it took the likes of Sean Hannity and Fox News, The Drudge Report, Alex Jones' Infowars, and one of the largest grassroots Conservative Networks: Grassfire, to promote and elevate the artist's status. Since that time, in addition to television and radio interviews, McNaughton continues to self-promote his work through appearances at conservative political conferences, such as CPAC and other opportune meetings and conventions that enable him to peddle his White Nationalist merchandise to Trump fans of all socioeconomic classes. Additionally, McNaughton is active on Twitter, where he advertises new and old works on an almost daily basis.

As a favorite and frequent guest of Sean Hannity, McNaughton has been able to reach a much broader audience to market his artistic wares, thereby increasing his own profit margin while providing imaginary cover for the president. Incidentally, Sean Hannity purchased an original, The Forgotten Man, for an estimated $300,000.00 to give to President Trump to hang in the White House. At a much-reduced cost, the McNaughton Fine Art Company recently offered an online special for an original Healing His Wings painting, available for purchase for a paltry $32,000.00, with litho prints starting at $29.00 and giclée prints priced up to $447.00 (McNaughton 2020).

For those on a more modest budget, the real bargains can be found on the McNaughton Fine Art Company's "Special Discount Page" (McNaughton 2020) that ensures that no grass-root Trump supporter is priced out of the art market. For those McNaughton fans on a much smaller budget than Sean Hannity, such as the growing number of unemployed Trump supporters without healthcare coverage during a deadly pandemic, the McNaughton Fine Art Company

---

6 In the span of less than a week while composing this paragraph on Trump Rushmore, McNaughton has released two new paintings for sale on his website: The Choice and Legacy of Hope.

generously offers more affordable prints that range between $29.00 and $705.00. McNaughton also offers deep-discounted "Jewelry," "Faith Packs," "Patriot Packs," "T-Shirts," and for coffee table art lovers, the McNaughton Fine Art Company also sells his very own retrospective art book of masterpieces for the low price of $100.00. Other deeply discounted items can be found on the website's "Specials" section, where McNaughton fans can also purchase exclusive "for a limited time" prints, such as Path of Peace: "Available to Facebook followers" (McNaughton 2020); and Friendly Halloween: "a Facebook special for those who love Halloween" (McNaughton 2020). While the McNaughton Fine Art Company's prints might not measure up to an original painting, McNaughton's "cheesy giclée prints,"[7] nevertheless, are affordable.

Arguably, McNaughton's art is the epitome of Marshall McLuhan's dictum: "The medium is the message." Indeed, McNaughton's paintings embody "the medium that shapes and controls the scale and form of human association and action" (McLuhan 1994, 196) through a growing catalog of far-right Republican reveries, earning the artist the creative sobriquet: "Glenn Beck with a paintbrush." (Oliaz and Duffy 2011) But perhaps McNaughton's modus operandi explains his lucrative success best; his uncanny ability to create appealing and triumphal Trumpian demagogical scenes, and peddle his works within a profitable online matrix where art meets mass-market propaganda ideologically hand-crafted for collectors and end consumers.

In defense of McNaughton, of course, he is not the only artist or entrepreneur to hitch his talents and fortunes to the Trump Train. Much in the way that the MAGA movement capitalizes on selling over-priced, made-in-China merchandise, McNaughton has found a lucrative niche market through the commercialization of right-wing propaganda. While a myriad of Asian manufacturers continues to mass-produce Trump merchandise in a long line of gauche products, what differentiates the McNaughton Fine Art Company's kitsch from its Asian competitors is that McNaughton's propaganda is proudly made in the U.S.A.

As reflected in McNaughton's continued hero-worship pattern, President Trump is—and is portrayed—as an American demigod for whom rules do not apply. Like many of his other works, McNaughton's growing catalog is Art for Public Instruction and Consumption, oil-based red meat for the deplorable masses. Thus, for the MAGA converted, McNaughton's artworks further fuel

---

[7] Christopher Knight suggests that McNaughton's giclée prints are nothing more than "a mass-market process akin to a high-tech version of your home computer's ink-jet printer. The process creates a simulation of paint on canvas. A giclée is an inauthentic painting, which is a pretty good description of McNaughton's One Nation Under Socialism" (Knight 2012).

Trump's cult of personality, glorifying an increasingly authoritarian leader in a nascent post-truth propaganda state where a president and a painter both profit on lies and deceit. In this respect, McNaughton simply another creative opportunist using his "God-given" talents to take full financial advantage of the promotions and propaganda marketplace for all things Trumpian.

And finally, taking into consideration recent polling data, with just a few months' away from the 2020 election, and McNaughton's prolific creative output as of late, it seems both Trump and his court painter share similar anxieties given the electoral prospect that the president might finally fall to his knees, not in prayer, of course. Perhaps McNaughton is coming to terms with the fact that his Trumpian "muse" might possibly lose the election. With McNaughton's income stream threatened then by a potential Trump loss, it is of little surprise that the artist is producing once- or twice-weekly portraits at a sweatshop pace in a final Trumpian yield, since his muse and moneymaker may no longer be objects of veneration and constant income. If Trump loses the election, however, McNaughton's fan base can rest assured that there will be a collection of anti-Joe Biden portraits offered on the McNaughton Fine Arts Company just in time for Christmas.

References

Arendt, Hannah. 1958. *The Origins of Totalitarianism.* New York: Meridian Books.

Baker, R. C. "MAGA Representing!: Send Jon McNaughton to the Venice Biennale!" The Village Voice. (Accessed: August 10, 2018). villagevoice.com/2018/08/10/maga-representing-send-painter-jon-mcnaughton-to-the-venice-biennale/

Castrodale, Jelisa. "Pro-Trump Kentucky BBQ Food Truck Faces Outrage Over "LGTBQ" T-Shirt." Vice. (Accessed: April 23, 2019). vice.com/en_us/article/evydyz/pro-trump-kentucky-bbq-food-truck-faces-outrage-over-lgbtq-t-shirts

Cole, Brendan. "Pastor Robert Jeffress Says Trump is Christian Warrior and Democrats Worship Pagan God Moloch "Who Allowed Child Sacrifice"." Newsweek. (Accessed: October 2, 2019). newsweek.com/robert-jeffress-donald-trump-defends-christians-todd-starnes-show-1462525

Coleman, Jonny. "8 Atrocious Examples of Modern American Conservative Art." LA Weekly. (Accessed: August 25, 2017). laweekly.com/8-atrocious-examples-of-modern-american-conservative-art/

Dafoe, Taylor. "Trump's State Department Had Yet to Pick a U.S. Representative for the Venice Biennale." ArtNetNews. (Accessed: July 27, 2018). news.artnet.com/art-world/should-this-pro-trump-painter-represent-the-us-at-next-years-venice-biennale-artist-justin-lieberman-suggests-hes-the-most-suited-for-the-role-1324724

Dreher, Rod. "A Fetid Journey with Swamp Things." The American Conservative. (Accessed: August 1, 2018). theamericanconservative.com/dreher/trump-crosses-the-swamp/

Encyclopedia Britannica. "Kneeling." Encyclopedia Britannica. (Accessed October 06, 2020). britannica.com/topic/kneeling

Fea, John. "Jon McNaughton a "Court Evangelical and a "Court Artist"?" The Way of Improvement Leads Home. (Accessed: October 15, 2019). thewayofimprovement.com/2019/10/15/is-jon-mcnaughton-a-court-evangelical-and-a-court-artist/

Gell, Aaron. "The Tea Party's Favorite Painter is Going Wobbly on Trump." Task & Purpose. (Accessed: May 13, 2017). taskandpurpose.com/lifestyle/tea-partys-favorite-painter-going-wobbly-trump

Hastings, Michael. "Anti-Obama Art Selling for Six-Figures." Buzz Feed News. (Accessed: April 3, 2012). buzzfeednews.com/article/mhastings/anti-obama-art-selling-for-six-figures

Hastings, Michael. "Anti-Obama Artist Strikes Again." Buzz Feed News. (Accessed: June 22, 2012). buzzfeednews.com/article/mhastings/anti-obama-artist-strikes-again

Hesse, Monica. "The Most Famous Pro-Trump Artist in the U.S. has Moved into His Mueller Phase." The Washington Post. (Accessed: May 15, 2018). washingtonpost.com/lifestyle/style/the-most-famous-pro-trump-artist-in-the-us-has-moved-into-his-mueller-phase/2018/05/15/6363a92e-552c-11e8-a551-5b648abe29ef_story.html

Jamitis, Jim. "Really Bad Art is No Way to Win Back the Culture." Red State. (Accessed: March 8, 2018). redstate.com/jimjamitis/2018/03/08/really-bad-art-no-way-win-back-culture/

Knight, Christopher. "Why Painting of President Obama with Burning Constitution is Junk." Los Angeles Times. (Accessed: March 26, 2012). latimesblogs.latimes.com/culturemonster/2012/03/why-a-painting-of-president-obama-with-a-burning-constitution-is-junk.html

McDonald, John. "When is Art Effective as Propaganda?" The Sydney Morning Herald. (Accessed: May 29, 2020). smh.com.au/culture/art-and-design/when-is-art-effective-as-propaganda-20200521-p54v5h.html

McLuhan, Marshall. 1994. *Understanding Media: The Extensions of Man.* Cambridge: MIT Press.

McNaughton, Jon. "2020 Ride." McNaughton Fine Art Company. (Accessed: June 21, 2020). jonmcnaughton.com/patriotic/americana/2020-ride/

McNaughton, Jon. "All-American Trump." McNaughton Fine Art Company. (Accessed: June 21, 2020). jonmcnaughton.com/patriotic/americana/all-american-trump/

McNaughton, Jon. "And Justice for All." McNaughton Fine Art Company. (Accessed: June 21, 2020). jonmcnaughton.com/copy-of-justice-for-all-18x24-limited-edition-litho-1500-s-n/

McNaughton, Jon. "Check Out." McNaughton Fine Art Company. (Accessed: June 21, 2020). jonmcnaughton.com/checkout.php

McNaughton, Jon. "Conservative Drawings." McNaughton Fine Art Company. (Accessed: June 21, 2020). jonmcnaughton.com/patriotic/conservative-drawings/

McNaughton, Jon. "Crossing the Swamp." McNaughton Fine Art Company. (Accessed: June 21, 2020). jonmcnaughton.com/crossing-the-swamp/

McNaughton, Jon. "Democrats Playing Poker." McNaughton Fine Art Company. (Accessed: June 21, 2020). jonmcnaughton.com/democrats-playing-poker/

McNaughton, Jon. "Expose the Truth." McNaughton Fine Art Company. (Accessed: June 21, 2020). jonmcnaughton.com/expose-the-truth/

McNaughton, Jon. "Friendly Halloween." McNaughton Fine Art Company. (Accessed: June 21, 2020). jonmcnaughton.com/friendly-halloween-facebook-special-p13/

McNaughton, Jon. "Healing His Wings." McNaughton Fine Art Company. (Accessed: May 19, 2019). jonmcnaughton.com/religious-gallery/religious/healing-in-his-wings/

McNaughton, Jon. "Legacy of Hope." McNaughton Fine Art Company. (Accessed: July 24, 2020). jonmcnaughton.com/legacy-of-hope/

McNaughton, Jon. "Liberalism is a Disease." McNaughton Fine Art Company. (Accessed: June 21, 2020). jonmcnaughton.com/liberalism-is-a-disease-by-jon-mcnaughton/

McNaughton, Jon. "Lincoln's Prayer." McNaughton Fine Art Company. (Accessed: June 21, 2020). jonmcnaughton.com/patriotic/americana/ lincolns-prayer/

McNaughton, Jon. "MAGA Ride." McNaughton Fine Art Company. (Accessed: June 21, 2020). jonmcnaughton.com/maga-ride/

McNaughton, Jon. "Make America Safe." McNaughton Fine Art Company. (Accessed: June 21, 2020). jonmcnaughton.com/patriotic/make-america-safe/

McNaughton, Jon. "Mending the Nation." McNaughton Fine Art Company. (Accessed: June 21, 2020). jonmcnaughton.com/patriotic/mending-the-nation/

McNaughton, Jon. "National Emergency." McNaughton Fine Art Company. (Accessed: June 21, 2020). jonmcnaughton.com/patriotic/national-emergency/

McNaughton, Jon. "Obama Foreign Policy." McNaughton Fine Art Company. (June 21, 2020). jonmcnaughton.com/patriotic/obama-foreign-policy/

McNaughton, Jon. "Obamanation." McNaughton Fine Art Company. (Accessed: June 21, 2020). jonmcnaughton.com/patriotic/obamanation/

McNaughton, Jon. "One Nation Under God." McNaughton Fine Art Company. (Accessed: June 21, 2020). https://jonmcnaughton.com/patriotic/americana/new-category/

McNaughton, Jon. "One Nation Under Socialism." McNaughton Fine Art Company. (Accessed: June 21, 2020). https://jonmcnaughton.com/patriotic/one-nation-under-socialism/

McNaughton, Jon. "Path of Peace." McNaughton Fine Art Company. (Accessed: June 21, 2020). https://jonmcnaughton.com/path-of-peace-18x22-le-facebook-special/

McNaughton, Jon. "Pray for America." McNaughton Fine Art Company. (Accessed: June 21, 2020). https://jonmcnaughton.com/patriotic/pray-for-america/

McNaughton, Jon. "Separation of Church and State." McNaughton Fine Art Company. (Accessed: June 21, 2020). https://jonmcnaughton.com/patriotic/separation-of-church-and-state/

McNaughton, Jon. "Specials." McNaughton Fine Art Company. (Accessed: June 21, 2020. https://jonmcnaughton.com/the-choice/)

McNaughton, Jon. "Teach a Man to Fish." McNaughton Fine Art Company. (Accessed: June 21, 2020). https://jonmcnaughton.com/patriotic/ americana/teach-a-man-to-fish/

McNaughton, Jon. "The Artist." McNaughton Fine Art Company. (Accessed: June 21, 2020). https://jonmcnaughton.com/the-artist/

McNaughton, Jon. "The Con Artist." McNaughton Fine Art Company. (Accessed: June 21, 2020). https://jonmcnaughton.com/patriotic/the-con-artist/

McNaughton, Jon. "The Demise of America." McNaughton Fine Art Company. (Accessed: June 21, 2020). https://jonmcnaughton.com/patriotic/the-demise-of-america/

McNaughton, Jon. "The Empowered Man." McNaughton Fine Art Company. (Accessed: June 21, 2020). https://jonmcnaughton.com/patriotic/the-empowered-man/

McNaughton, Jon. "The Forgotten Man." McNaughton Fine Art Company. (Accessed: June 21, 2020). https://jonmcnaughton.com/patriotic/the-forgotten-man/

McNaughton, Jon. "The Impeachment Mob." McNaughton Fine Art Company. (Accessed: June 21, 2020). https://jonmcnaughton.com/patriotic/americana/the-impeachment-mob/

McNaughton, Jon. "The Masterpiece." McNaughton Fine Art Company. (Accessed: June 21, 2020). https://jonmcnaughton.com/the-masterpiece-24x30-canvas-giclee-s-n-100/

McNaughton, Jon. "The Resistance." McNaughton Fine Art Company. (Accessed: June 21, 2020). https://jonmcnaughton.com/patriotic/the-resistance/

McNaughton, Jon. "Trump Rushmore." McNaughton Fine Art Company. (Accessed: July 20, 2020). https://jonmcnaughton.com/trump-rushmore/

McNaughton, Jon. "Wake Up America." McNaughton Fine Art Company. (Accessed: June 21, 2020). https://jonmcnaughton.com/patriotic/wake-up-america/

McNaughton, Jon. "Washington's Prayer." McNaughton Fine Art Company. (Accessed: June 21, 2020). https://jonmcnaughton.com/patriotic/washingtons-prayer/

McNaughton, Jon. "You Are Fake News." McNaughton Fine Art Company. (Accessed: June 21, 2020). https://jonmcnaughton.com/you-are-fake-news-10x15-litho/

McNaughton, Jon. "You Are Not Forgotten." McNaughton Fine Art Company. (Accessed: June 21, 2020). jonmcnaughton.com/you-are-not-forgotten-16x24-inch-open-edition-print-signed/

Milbank, Dana. "Trump Claims He's the Messiah. Maybe He Should Quit While He's Ahead." The Washington Post. (Accessed: August 21, 2019). washingtonpost.com/opinions/trump-claims-hes-the-messiah-maybe-he-should-quit-while-hes-ahead/2019/08/21/4eb6bdcc-c44d-11e9-b5e4-54aa56d5b7ce_story.html

Montgomery, Peter. "Robert Jeffress: America is a 'Christian Nation' Whose Constitution Has Been Perverted by Secularists and 'Infidels'." Right Wing Watch. (Accessed: July 14, 2020). rightwingwatch.org/post/robert-jeffress-america-is-a-christian-nation-whose-constitution-has-been-perverted-by-secularists-and-infidels/?fbclid=IwAR3uHyLbkcQD9QTuGKBZnLaEQ2tRLzXimVOt-vqwam2RWbjZUo6Jgok-UQc

Morgan, David. "The Art of Jon McNaughton, the Tea Party's Painter." Religion & Politics. (Accessed: July 25, 2012). religionandpolitics.org/2012/07/25/the-tea-partys-painter-the-art-of-jon-mcnaughton/

Mormon Wiki. "John McNaughton." Mormon Wiki. (Accessed October 06, 2020). mormonwiki.com/Jon_McNaughton

Oliaz, Hugo, and John-Charles Duffy. "Painting Up Controversy: The Work of Jon McNaughton." Sunstone Magazine. (Accessed: October 31, 2011). sunstonemagazine.com/painting-up-controversy-the-work-of-jon-mcnaughton/

Perry, Elder L. T. "God's Hand in the Founding of America." The Church of Jesus Christ of Latter-Day Saints. (Last updated: February 24, 1976). churchofjesuschrist.org/study/new-era/1976/07/gods-hand-in-the-founding-of-america?lang=eng

Perticone, John. "Conservative Artists Jon McNaughton Doesn't Care About the Haters, He Just Wants to Paint Trump and Jesus." Business Insider. (Accessed: August 5, 2018). businessinsider.com/jon-mcnaughton-is-the-maga-movements-most-celebrated-artist-2018-8

Rees, Robert. 2012. "Love and the Christian imagination." *Keynote Devotional, Affirmation National Conference.* Seattle.

Rodgers, Jennifer. "Finally, the Supreme Court Can Tell Trump He's Not Above the Law." CNN Opinion. (Accessed: May 13, 2020). cnn.com/2020/05/13/opinions/supreme-court-trump-tax-returns-rodgers/index.html

Shapiro, Eliza. "Anti-Obama Paintings Selling for $300,000." New York Magazine. (Accessed: April 3, 2012). nymag.com/intelligencer/2012/04/anti-obama-paintings-selling-for-300000.html

Substack, Jeb. "Trump, Burt and Loni (Oil on Canvas, 2019): The Very Beautiful, Very Exclusive Religion of Presidential Art." The End of the Peninsula. (Accessed: March 7, 2019). jeb.substack.com/p/trump-burt-and-loni-oil-on-canvas

Taggart, Emma. "The Story Behind the Iconic "Dogs Playing Poker" Paintings." My Modern Met. (Accessed: October 06, 2020). mymodernmet.com/dogs-playing-poker-painting/

Tait, Joshua. "Make Art Great Again?: Artist and Trump Superfan Jon McNaughton, Conservatives, Painting, and Americana." Arc Digital Media. (Accessed: June 11, 2019). arcdigital.media/this-april-jon-mcnaughton-the-unofficial-artist-of-the-trump-administration-unveiled-his-7350147815dd

Tani, Maxwell. "Trump on God: 'I Don't Like to Have to Ask for Forgiveness'." Business Insider. (Accessed: January 17, 2016). businessinsider.com/trump-on-god-i-dont-like-to-have-to-ask-for-forgiveness-2016-1

Uglow, Jenny. "When Art Meets Power." New York Review of Books. (Accessed: March 8, 2017). nybooks.com/daily/2017/03/08/when-art-meets-power-russia-revolution/

Weist, Ellen F. "A Provo Artist Painted President Donald Trump Clutching an American Flag on a Football Field. The Internet Reacted Accordingly." The Salt Lake Tribune, (Accessed: March 1, 2018). sltrib.com/news/2018/02/27/

provo-patriotic-painter-jon-mcnaughton-gets-a-boost-from-sean-hannity-but-art-critics-scoff/

Wolfe, Matthew. "The Right's Shepherd Fairey." Salon. (Accessed: February 9, 2012). salon.com/2012/02/09/the_rights_shepard_fairey/

Zoom, Doktor. "Great American Artist, Jon McNaughton Being Accidental Nazi, Again." Wonkette. (Accessed: June 14, 2018). wonkette.com/great-american-artist-jon-mcnaughton-cries-finish-the-damn-picket-fence

About the Authors

Kevin Xiong

Kevin Xiong is a growth strategist, management consultant, and multimedia artist. Kevin currently leads growth at Truveta, a healthcare technology company with a mission to save lives with data. Prior to Truveta, he advised Fortune 500 leaders on growth strategy, performance improvement, customer experience, and organizational design at McKinsey & Company, a management consulting firm. Kevin serves as a Board member of several non-profits, including the Charity of Edward Hopkins, wayOUT Bay Area, and Breakthrough Greater Boston. His former experiences include Artsy and J.P. Morgan.

Kevin graduated *magna cum laude* from Harvard College with a Bachelor of Arts in Economics and a secondary in the Mathematical Sciences and was a John Eliot Scholar at the University of Cambridge, where he earned a Master of Philosophy in Asian and Middle Eastern Studies with a dissertation on Beijing's 798 Art Zone. He is also a practitioner of the arts, as an award-winning painter, singer-songwriter, and producer. You can view his work at www.kevinxiong.com.

Marek Prokůpek

Marek Prokůpek is Assistant Professor of Arts Management, Cultural Economics, and Art Markets at the Prague University of Economics and Business. From 2018 to 2020, he was a Postdoctoral Fellow at the LabEx ICCA (Industries culturelles et création artistique) in Paris. Marek's research interests are primarily in the areas of museum fundraising and philanthropy and its ethical aspects and dilemmas, arts finance, performance measurement and innovative business models of arts and cultural organizations. In addition, he focuses on the issue of museum observatories and statistics. Dr. Prokůpek has held the position of visiting professor at the KEDGE Business School in Paris and Bordeaux, where he has lectured on the finances of arts and culture and the art market. As part of his doctoral degree in Arts Management, successfully completed in March 2017, he conducted research on the performance measurement of public art museums. He spent part of his doctoral studies in Paris at the Université Paris III Sorbonne-Nouvelle as visiting researcher in the Department of Médiation Culturelle.

Irini Liakopoulou

Irini Liakopoulou currently works as Professor of Finance at the State Oklahoma University, and she is part-time Professor of Macroeconomics at the Union College-NY. She has also worked in several European universities in the past and published various books, mainly in the fields of macroeconomics, European economics and public economics.

Vladan Kuzmanovic

Vladan Kuzmanovic is an academic economist, theoretician, avant-garde artist and polymath. He is a member of the New York Marketing Association, The Association of Strategic Marketing, The American Communication Association, and The Society for the Study of the History of Analytical Philosophy, among others. His research fields are Marketing, Behavior Science, Consumer Behavior, Management, Advertising, Economic Theory, Environmental Management, with a special interest in Conceptual Marketing and Applied Behavior.

Gladys Pierpauli

Gladys Pierpauli has an MA in Sociology of Culture (ABD), National University of San Martín (UNSAM), Argentina. She is a professor of television studies at Instituto Superior de Ensenanza Radiofonica (ISER), Argentina. Pierpauli is also a journalist and media consultant and part of Argentina's National Public Radio (Radio Nacional Argentina). She has published on global cultural topics in books: "Heterotopia and Globalisation in the Twenty-First Century" (Routledge) and journals: "Argentine Film Representation of Chinese(ness)" (Glocalism).

Mariano Turzi

Mariano Turzi has a Ph.D. in International Studies from the School of Advanced International Studies (SAIS), Johns Hopkins University. He is a professor at UCEMA and the Austral University. He has co-written a book on China (Palgrave) and several journal articles (Yale Journal of International Affairs, Journal of Latin American Studies of the Chinese Academy of Social Sciences).

Aritra De

Aritra De is currently a Ph.D. candidate and a Teaching Assistant in the Department of History at Texas Tech University. He completed his master's and bachelor's degree from Jadavpur University, India. He is doing his research on the impact of the Cold War on the Socio-Political and Cultural Sphere of West Bengal.

Nat Hardy

Nat Hardy is the Founding Dean of Arts and Humanities and the Sara Jane Johnson Scholar at Stephens College in Columbia, Missouri. Nat has over twenty years' experience in supporting higher education through his current role as Dean of Arts and Humanities, and former roles as Associate Dean of Arts, Sciences & Professional Studies, Director of Graduate Studies, Director of the Honors Program, Director of Online Education, Chair of the Department of Liberal Arts, and as a full professor of Literature, Creative Writing, and Humanities. Nat possesses a record of Humanities research and service with substantial publications, creative works and presentations in professional venues. He also has editorial experience with arts and literature journals and has served on the mastheads of The New Delta Review, Nimrod: International Journal of Prose and Poetry, The Exquisite Corpse, the Cimarron Review and New Writing: International Journal for Theory and Practice of Creative Writing.

Nat holds a Ph.D. in the Early Modern Literature of Illness and Disease (University of Alberta), an M.Ed. in Higher Education Administration (Georgia Southern University), an M.F.A. in Creative Writing (Louisiana State University), an M.A. in Restoration Utopian Literature (McMaster University) and a B.A. in Literature and Philosophy (University of Alberta).

To date, Nat has held teaching and administrative positions at the Stephens College, the College of Saint Mary, Savannah State University, Rogers State University, Oklahoma State University, Louisiana State University, the University of Alberta and McMaster University, and has earned numerous awards for his teaching and service. Most recently, he was elected a Fellow of the Royal Society of Arts (RSA) in London, England, and currently serves on the Board of Directors of the Missouri Humanities Council. He also is the proud father of his eleven-year-old daughter, Madeline Hardy.

Index

N

P

R

S

T

U

www.ingramcontent.com/pod-product-compliance
Lightning Source LLC
LaVergne TN
LVHW010721210926
848485LV00007B/1403/J
* 9 7 8 1 6 4 8 8 9 0 4 8 2 *